THE SAVVY GUIDE TO BUYING BURIAL INSURANCE

What you need to know before you meet with your agent

AL KUSHNER

The Savvy Guide to Buying Burial Insurance – What You Need to Know Before You Talk to the Right Agent by Al Kushner

This publication is designed to provide accurate and authoritative information in regard to the subject matter covered. It is sold with the understanding that the publisher and author is not engaged in rendering psychological, financial, legal, or other professional services. If legal advice, expert assistance, or counseling is needed, the services of a competent professional should be sought.

Published by SCR Media Inc, Box 7103, Delray Beach, Fl 33482

www.SuperiorMutual.com

For information about special discounts available for bulk purchases, sales promotions, fund-raising and educational needs, contact SCR Media Inc Sales at 1-561-909-6975 or scrbooks@gmail.com

ISBN 9781632273208   EBOOK ISBN 9781632273192

First Edition

MY GIFT TO YOU!

Thank you for purchasing this book. As a token of my appreciation, I'm giving you a FREE 40-page special report:

Colonial Penn, Globe Life, Lincoln Heritage, Mutual of Omaha & AARP Burial Insurance – Are These Companies A Rip-Off?

Discover the secrets that they don't want you to know in my free special report now!

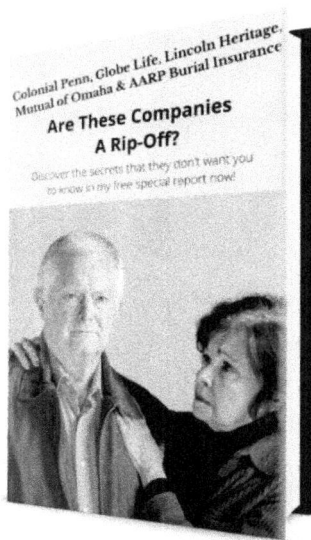

Get it here at https://BookHip.com/XLBBNX

or scan qr code below

PRAISE

"Do not go anywhere else for your own final expense needs on this kind of policy. This was really easy, and you'll be provided ample opportunity to ask lots of questions and get your needs fulfilled. Good feeling knowing you're in good hands with a professional that's been an agent since 1986, understands his business inside and outside, has many carriers to pick from, and a seamless application process. I especially liked the fact that I had been on the telephone with broker and insurer and managed to listen to what occurred and fix any information I could have stated incorrect like cell number, home address, social, etc. Worth waiting to speak to Al and the process was finished in expedited manner. Delighted that I was able to buy two policies together with the same broker." **Deja J – Waco, TX**

"Al Kushner was amazing at helping with obtaining insurance for my elderly father. He had term insurance with New York Life AARP, which he did outlive from the age 80. I tried to renew his insurance with New York Life, and I could not believe how inexperienced the agent was with the process. I was recommended by a friend to call Superior Mutual. I was really pleased with the whole process. I would strongly recommend them for your insurance needs. They will help you through the challenges of insuring an elderly parent, and they are not pushy! Thanks again." - **Jamal B – Summerville, SC**

"I was able to be approved for the life insurance I desired, not in days, but immediately over the telephone. I received a hard copy of the policy within a week. Al was knowledgeable, helpful and extremely kind. I would not hesitate to recommend Superior Mutual to anybody interested in obtaining life insurance for your first time or for obtaining additional coverage." - **John R -Akron, OH**

"Al was quite helpful in obtaining insurance for me. I had been looking at a guaranteed insurance policy because other agents told me that was the only way I could get coverage. It turns out that wasn't true, but Al got me the coverage I wanted, and it was really affordable. It was also a whole life insurance policy

and began immediately. He answered all our questions and created what was becoming a very difficult endeavor, very simple and hassle-free." – **Jacob C –**
El Paso, TX

"I'd just bought an individual life policy with a 2-year waiting period. However, I was calling around to determine if this was the best option and Al Kushner from Superior Mutual was my contact. I explained to him that I had already gotten a policy and upon asking some additional questions and a few phone calls later he managed to find me coverage for my husband which was much better than the one I had selected on my own. He was quite knowledgeable, thorough and very good at what he does. He ended up getting me a policy that had no waiting period. The price was great! We are very happy so if anyone needs assistance with life insurance, I recommend this company and this agent." -
Jazmine H – Key West, FL

"After exploring quotes from quite a few other companies, I went with Superior Mutual. . .Initially because of their affiliation with several reputable businesses such as Mutual of Omaha. Gerber and Prosperity, which have a good reputation of integrity & service spanning over 100 decades, also since they had a much more affordable rate for a male non-smoker within my age range. Including many other considerate advantages not available with the other businesses. And I must admit, interacting with agents can be sometimes daunting, but after a few minutes discussion with Al Kushner I KNEW I had made the right decision! He is very kind & educated, and a genuine "people-person". He clarified & walked me through the procedure. He was very patient and got me exactly what I needed. He is a fantastic all-around perfect example of what a TRUE agent ought to be! I HIGHLY RECOMMEND Superior Mutual (AND Al) with this real "Peace of Mind" insurance!" – **Jackson H –**
Florence, SC

"Al Kushner was helpful in making proper choices myself. Simply explained what I needed in a policy and health scenarios that would cause specific companies to turn me down. Al found a carrier with a highly competitive rate for my situation in less than 30 seconds. He guided me through the interview process on a 3-way call with the insurance carrier. Great follow up from Al. Let me know I was approved and answered any questions I had about coverage.

Al also discovered a replacement policy for my partner at a more affordable monthly price. Would certainly use this service again." - **Trevon A- Austin, TX**

"Mr. Kushner was one of several that I priced term life insurance with. Being 67 put me in a class of paying over $200 a month for $100,000 ten-year term policy, even with firms used by AARP. The policy I managed to acquire through Mr. Kushner did not increase cost with each fifth-year birthdays, which is what AARP's did. By the 75th birthday AARP premium could have been under $300 monthly; however, it would end at the 75th birthday. The coverage I was able to buy was with AIG, a company started and still headquarter in my home state. My premium is $134.00 per month for the duration of 20 years and cannot be cancelled by the company. Obviously, this was hundreds below what I expected to pay. I could not be happier! "– **Emanuel L – Brooklyn NY**

"Al Kushner took approximately 90 minutes to talk through my life scenario, my objectives, and my wishes to make sure I applied for the coverage amount and policy that were best for my wife and me. He answered all my queries, followed up promptly, and followed through on all he promised. Al was the 4th representative I had spoken with and he had been infinitely more helpful and knowledgeable than the other people I had talked with. Before retirement, I used to manage a team of insurance agents and Al was more professional and educated than any agent I have ever worked with. Al is the real McCoy and will make sure that you're taken care of correctly! "- **Darnell T – Dayton, OH**

"Al Kushner really does a great job writing a great book geared for consumers on the under-reported benefits of cash value life insurance. Straight forward and gets to the point without a whole lot of stories that can be boring. I recommend this book for anyone who is in the accounting services industry with clients who do not understand the importance of taking care of one's final expense. It could be a life changer for how you do business and for your client as well. The author truly understands how to hold a person's attention." -**Marie Torosian CPA**

DEDICATION

You know how it is. You pick up a book, flip to the dedication, and find that, once again, the author has dedicated a book to someone else and not you.

Not this time.

Because we have not yet met/have only a glancing acquaintance/are just crazy about each other/haven't seen each other in much too long/are in some way related/will never meet, but will, I trust, despite that, always think fondly of each other...

This one's for you.

With you know what, and you probably know why.

Contents

FOREWORD

Over the years, talking about mortality has been taboo because it causes distress in most human beings. An impressive aspect that I learned in practice when working as a general practitioner was to value life. My face was the first one that many saw at birth, and I was the one who accompanied some when they died. Today, since retired, I remember several of the things I experienced, and a fundamental aspect of human existence that I managed to understand is that we are fragile.

Even though today's medicine is of high quality, every Doctor knows that it has its limits; we must understand the link between illness and death. There is also a close statistical relationship between some conditions and exposure to harmful factors; that is, many people would not be sick if they had taken adequate precautions. Some of these problems, such as substance abuse, obesity, AIDS, hepatitis B, among others, could affect an individual's longevity.

I remember a young patient who came to the emergency room seriously injured after being in a car accident. He once told me, "Doctor, I never thought this could happen to me; I felt very safe and healthy, in my head, it was possible for others, I was confident in my skills, and I thought that something like this would never happen to a guy like me." I remember that, fortunately, he managed to save himself and left after a long and painful recovery. The life lesson he left me was essential but straightforward; most people think that illness and accidents happen to others. Another young man in his 30s, who was not so lucky, was the father of a beautiful baby and had an excellent wife. He looked away from the wheel for a second to answer a call from his boss, the accident was fatal, and he was not prepared. The widow had to deal with the expense of a dignified burial; The stress added to the pain, and it ended up being a doubly tragic experience for a humble middle-class family.

According to the CDC, life expectancy in the United States is 78.7 years. Of course, these are general figures, and many individual factors can influence the fact that some will live short while others will enjoy a long existence. Another vital factor to consider is that, as we age, health problems appear to become very difficult and expensive to insure. Many of the Baby Boomers and retirees have not had the good fortune of being free from their obligations and with enough savings to cover their debts, final expenses, and other commitments.

Life insurance is a basic form of insurance that will allow us to take care of those we love if we die if it has conditions and exclusions. Both the costs of this and the amount of coverage depend on multiple factors such as medical history, age, gender, and lifestyle. When benefits are paid, the agreed sum of money is given to the beneficiary. Being positive is transcendental in daily life. However, this attitude must be accompanied by a little caution. It is the wisdom of being balanced, having the advantage of sleeping peacefully every day, sure of knowing that, if something happens to us, the family will be able to focus on the duel and the rest will be resolved.

Some factors can increase the value of premiums so that some lifestyle changes can decrease the cost significantly. Currently, many companies insure sick people either for life insurance or for funeral expenses as you qualify; however, we will analyze the measures that can be taken to lower the cost of premiums paid monthly or annually:

Smoking:

According to the Center for Disease Control and Prevention, known by its acronym in CDC, more than 16 million Americans suffer from a disease caused by smoking. Research has shown that smoking causes cancer, heart disease, stroke, diabetes, and lung disease, including Chronic Obstructive Pulmonary Disease (COPD), chronic bronchitis, and emphysema. For all the above, insurance companies consider and classify smokers as high-risk clients because, as you have already seen, they have a high probability of developing life-threatening diseases. Therefore, we recommend that you stop smoking as soon as possible. By quitting for 12 months in a row, you will be able to enjoy a healthier life, save a lot of money you used to spend on cigarettes, improve your life expectancy, and reduce the cost of your insurance policy premiums.

Morbid Obesity

Many factors currently contribute to morbid obesity, such as sedentary life and excess high-calorie products available in the market. According to the CDC, obesity predisposes to type 2 diabetes, cardiovascular disease, gastrointestinal disease, stroke, cancer, etc., which indicates that many premature deaths are preventable. That is why we recommend improving your diet, exercising, and being evaluated by a doctor because diseases cause obesity, such as hypothyroidism, side effects of the intake of certain medications, among others. Anyone suffering from morbid obesity will be classified as high risk by life insurance companies, increasing the premiums' cost. By improving your diet and exercising, you will not only enhance your lifestyle, but you will pay less for your insurance.

Alcohol

Without a doubt, alcohol is harmful to your health. According to statistical data from the CDC, alcoholism was responsible for the death of 1 in 10 deaths of adults of working age, that is, in individuals who were between 20 and 64 years old. According to this same entity, the effects of acute poisoning could cause sudden deaths related to accidents, violence and risky sexual behaviors that could eventually cause sexually transmitted diseases such as AIDS and Hepatitis b.

In the long term, your life would be in danger because abuse can cause psychiatric problems (anxiety and depression), nervous system diseases (memory and sleep problems), high blood pressure, certain types of cancer (breast, liver, colon), liver cirrhosis among many other diseases.

It should be noted that the liver is an essential organ for human life. Its critical role includes metabolizing drugs and eliminate toxic products. It has a significant role in absorbing some vitamins and fat; it produces proteins such as those involved in blood clotting and plays a fundamental role in extracting nutrients absorbed by the digestive system from the blood.

Diseases such as hepatitis B and alcoholism, among many others, can cause liver cirrhosis, which involves architectural damage because functional tissue is damaged by the process of chronic inflammation of the liver. This results in the appearance of fibrous tissue (scars), leading, in most cases, to an irreversible and progressive deterioration. It can be asymptomatic for many years; however, the prognosis is poor when the disease begins to manifest. According to statistical data reported by the American College of Gastroenterology, liver cirrhosis is the seventh leading cause of death in the United States in working-age adults.

Acquired Immune Deficiency Syndrome (AIDS)

AIDS is a disease that attacks by weakening the immune system, making those who suffer from it predispose to some types of cancer such as Kaposi's sarcoma and to multiple infections that generally would not affect healthy individuals. Caused by HIV (Human Immunodeficiency Virus), it is **transmitted through body fluids** and being more common through sexual intercourse. Also, the use of contaminated needles (as occurs in drug addiction) and procedures such as tattoos made by people who are not adequately trained or possess the necessary equipment to provide a safe method for their clients. The risk of contamination through blood transfusion has decreased significantly as donors are routinely tested today.

According to the CDC, in 2018, 37,968 people were diagnosed with HIV in the United States for a total of 1.2 million cases. A significant fact is that 1 in 7 did not know they had the infection. This statistic is vital because some people infect others without knowing they have the disease. It should be noted that the proper and responsible use of antiretrovirals, that is, the treatments for this disease, will allow you to live longer and better and reduce the risk of contagion to your sexual partners to a minimum. The problem is, and I reiterate, that many have not been diagnosed or treated while others do not follow the treatment to the letter; this condition remains incurable and could affect the cost of insurance. Proper counseling will help you find the best **insurance** opportunities despite suffering from this disease.

Opioids

They are substances highly used for pain that can cause Opioid Use Disorder (diagnosed according to DMS-5 criteria) and overdose. This resulted in more than 20,000 people deaths in 2015, and heroin overdoses caused another 12,990. These substances can be highly addictive because they eliminate the pain and induce euphoria due primarily to Mu receptors' stimulation; However, the process is much more complicated. It involves inhibition of neurons in specific brain pathways, thus causing sedation, analgesia, respiratory depression, and reinforcement for the drug's use, among other things. Over time it can cause tolerance, that is, the need for a higher dose to achieve the same effect. Many sellers of illegal drugs use this to sell more potent substances such as fentanyl or others cheaper than those prescribed, such as heroin. The use of needles for the latter predisposes to diseases such as AIDS and hepatitis B. Fatal overdose is a common complication of substance use disorder due to respiratory depression, bradycardia, and Central Nervous System depression.

Avoiding risk factors like those mentioned above is an excellent practice for your quality of life and your financial well-being. Everything explained increases the costs of medical services and your policies. I recommend an expert like Al Kushner, who can guarantee you the lowest prices and best carriers with his 35+ years of experience in the insurance industry. In the end, it will be an excellent investment and peace of mind.

Carol Trejos M.D.

A Beginner's Guide to Burial Insurance

Many senior citizens and their families do not know about burial insurance, but it could potentially be exactly what they need. If you had seen or heard the terms final expense insurance or funeral insurance, what you're looking at is burial insurance. Though used interchangeably, they all mean the same thing: a form of life insurance that purely covers funeral costs to ensure the bereaved are not financially burdened.

Unlike some life insurance policies, burial insurance plans never expire, never increase their monthly premiums, and never require a medical exam. Should a company ever say otherwise, they are flat out wrong. If you have been rejected from life insurance, need more coverage, or have medical bills to pay off in addition to final expenses, burial insurance might be your answer.

In this article, we will go through how burial insurance works explicitly, what to look out for, and how to make sure you or your loved one gets the best policy for them.

Let's Start by Describing the Process

When the insured loved one passes away the carrier cuts a tax-free check to the beneficiary to pay for final expenses. There are no restrictions or provisions for how the money is to be used. Any proceeds left over after costs have been paid to stay with the beneficiary. In a way, a burial insurance plan can be a financial legacy.

Now, there are three main options in burial insurance:

- **Level Benefit**

- **Graded**

- **Guaranteed Issue**

Note: There is another option called a modified plan. These plans are deemed by many reputable agencies to be utterly worthless. The three being described are what you should consider. Stay away from modified plans.

The policy you fall under depends on a variety of factors. Some companies' policies may not be approved in every state and have stipulations about age and your level of health. Perhaps the most critical factor throughout the industry is the number and severity of health conditions.

Most companies have three categories of health ratings that will determine the policy itself and the cost: low, medium, or high. This rating is determined by a detailed series of mandated health questions called medical underwriting for the level of benefit and graded plans. Don't be alarmed; it is not an exam – more like a questionnaire where you answer honestly about any illnesses you have.

This is a process unique to final expense insurance. It will encompass a wide range of conditions so people with high-risk illnesses can still secure coverage. It includes diabetic neuropathy, cholesterol issues, home health care, Parkinson's, depression, MS, high blood pressure, mini strokes, all kinds of arthritis, sleep apnea, fibromyalgia, atrial fibrillation, asthma, cystic fibrosis, schizophrenia, blood clots, and much more.

Let's go deeper in-depth about each category of burial insurance to determine where you may qualify. Level benefit plans equal to the low or "preferred" rating. If your health is relatively good and you have no severe conditions, this is the plan you will most likely fall under. From day one, you will receive full benefits and coverage from the lowest cost because you are not labeled what the carrier would call a 'great risk'.

Level benefit plans equal to the low or "preferred" rating. If your health is relatively good and you have no severe conditions, this is the plan you will most likely fall under. From day one, you will receive full benefits and coverage from the lowest cost because you are not labeled what the carrier would call a 'great risk'.

Graded plans are the 'medium' rating if the company does three ratings instead of two. This is the option you may be offered if you answer yes to some of the health questions in the graded section of the questionnaire. There is a 24-month waiting period for full benefits, meanwhile, you will receive partial coverage that increases the following year. Most companies will pay out around 30% if the insured passes away during the first year and 40-70% during the second. Prosperity and Lincoln Heritage are two companies that rate well in level benefit and graded plans.

Guarantee issue plans are a lifesaver for those with health risks or multiple conditions insurance companies deem the highest liability and refuse to consider. Some companies specialize in these plans for this very reason. Essentially, if you can enter into a legal contract, you are going to be accepted. These policies include, but are not limited to, people who have dialysis, Alzheimer's, dementia, severe epilepsy, have had recent cancer treatment, or are in hospice care or a nursing facility. Since there is no underwriting required, carriers do not know what risks they are taking on and therefore have to compensate with higher prices, and there will **always** be a two-year graded period. Should the insured person pass away during this time frame, premiums are paid back in full plus 10%, so at least no matter what happens, you will be getting more out of the plan than you put in. Accidental deaths, however, are covered from day one, which in some cases, like seizures or dementia, can, unfortunately, be very important. Once the two-year period has expired, you will receive full coverage and benefits. Some companies well known for these particular plans are Gerber Life Insurance, Sons of Norway and Great Western.

It is worth noting that, excluding the guarantee issue, companies will also look at your prescription history when determining your plan to validate the application's answers during the medical underwriting portion of the application. This will not require a printed-out list from your pharmacy or any extra phone calls/work on your part – with your consent; the company can electronically analyze your medications in a matter of minutes.

No Matter What You or Your Loved One's Health Condition May Be, There Will Always be a Policy Available. Do Not Let a Company or Agent Tell You Otherwise.

A unique aspect of burial insurance is the broad range of face values you can purchase, so you don't have to spend more than is necessary. Most companies range from about $2,000-$25,000, but some companies offer as little as $1,000. If you want a cremation, generally from $2,000-$5,000 for everything to be covered – that is all you need to pay for. Therefore, do not feel pressured into paying for a more expensive policy than you know is necessary– the amount you want is sure to be available to you.

Now that we've discussed the variety of plans and what carriers require let's move on to securing a policy.

Most companies in this industry will not allow you to call them and sign up directly – they will tell you to find an agent. This may seem strange, but it could work in your favor if you find the right person. An agent's job is essentially to do your shopping for you: after evaluating your health, they determine which companies work best for you and then find the cheapest policies to suit your needs. From there, you discuss which option to pursue.

Because burial insurance is such a niche industry with many stipulations regarding health conditions, it's best to find an agent specializing in final expenses. A 'jack of all trades' may not know all the specificities that go into finding a policy for someone who's had a recent heart attack, for instance. They could push the wrong plan on you when you qualify for better. It is also vital that the agency represents at least ten to fifteen different insurance companies to ensure various options and costs are being examined. Most importantly, do your research before making any final choices or giving out personal information. Look for good reviews from other customers to certify their credibility and trustworthiness. Levinson and Associates has a reputable reputation as an agency, as does Superior Mutual.

Under the guidance of your agent, you will submit your application to the selected company (another reason why you want an experienced agent working with you), typically done in one of three ways:

- Voice

- Email

- Paper

Voice and email are the most common ways to apply, but the paper does happen occasionally.

Submitting through voice means everything is done over the phone, even signatory authorizations. No paperwork is involved, it usually only takes a couple of minutes, and a decision often happens right then and there. Royal Neighbors of America, an excellent final expense company that takes on many high-risk patients, uses voice signature. Prosperity Life is another well- known carrier that uses vocal authorization for applications.

For email submissions, your agent collects all the information for you, and the company sends over an email to sign the whole thing in a couple of steps. Think of it as the tablets handed to you when seeing a new doctor so you can sign the appropriate disclosure and privacy agreements. Once you sign, you will be prompted with the medical underwriting portion (unless it is a guarantee issue). Decisions are usually made within a week. Mutual of Omaha, a company known for its level benefit and graded policies, do instant approval via email.

Paper applications essentially mean snail mail. Again, your agent collects everything necessary, generates the papers for you, and then sends it to your address. All you have to do is sign them and return them to your agent, where they'll take care of the rest. Decisions are made within five business days.

Everything seems straightforward, right? You know what burial insurance means, the types of plans available, the policies you might qualify for, and how to snag a reputable agent to help you with the whole process. So why does insurance have such a bad name? Why are insurance scams, particularly in the burial industry, so familiar?

Let's walk through some of the more prevalent final expense deceptions and how you can easily spot them.

First of all, be aware of how companies (and agents) may market burial insurance to increase prices or set you with the wrong policy. As stated earlier, burial insurance could be presented to you as final expenses or funeral insurance. They're the same.

Also, be on the lookout for companies trying to pass off term life insurance as burial expenses. AARP and Global Life, for instance, are notorious for marketing in just such a way. The AARP burial plan can be marketed as a state-regulated life insurance policy, or, can be a term life insurance policy. These plans carry vastly different meanings, which, if not thoroughly understood, can come at a great price, and possibly leave you without coverage when you most need it.

Term life insurance has an expiration date, most commonly when you're 80. These plans make sense if, say, a young family that is just starting and can't afford the costlier payments that come with permanent policies but plan on being able to afford it later in their lives. That way should something happen to either one or both of them before a permanent plan is in place, the surviving members of the family are being looked after accordingly and don't incur additional or remaining debt. You want to start permanent plans as young as possible, because the younger you start, the cheaper the monthly premiums as long as you don't cancel.

You could be 55 and still pay the same amount you did at 30. So though the lower prices might be appealing to you (mostly if it's marketed as burial insurance), once you reach a certain age, it's no longer worth it. As evidenced in the name, term life insurance policies are not meant to be permanent – so using it to cover final expenses just doesn't work. If you're sold one of these policies, say at 60, thinking it's a burial plan, once you turn 80, not only will you be left without coverage, but you won't get any money back.

The monthly premiums you were paying disappear into the insurance company's pocket. Should you attempt to renew, the premiums would increase every five years. Because the plan isn't permanent, the company wants to keep making money while they still can. Either you'll be paying up to 300% more, or you won't be able to pay, and the coverage will lapse. Always read the literature, fine print and all, given to you by the agent and company to make sure you're not purchasing the entirely wrong kind of life insurance policy.

Some websites and companies will offer seemingly incredible prices that are either scams or frauds. It's best never to buy a no-questions-asked policy from TV advertisements: there is bound to be plenty of fine print you would never see, and yet still be under obligation to pay exorbitant rates compared to what the ad sells you. This is pretty much the same way scam websites operate – they'll offer immediate sign up with the lowest prices on the market – except they're purely facades to steal your credit card/bank information, not in any way insurance. Remember, any reputable company would work with your agent, not allow you to directly sign up and pay on a website or over the phone.

However, when you make your payments, always pay directly to the company, not your agent. If your agent asks for cash to be delivered to them or a check to be made in their name, find another agent as soon as possible. They most likely want to pocket the money for themselves or at least a large portion of it.

All of this information may be overwhelming and somewhat scary, but as long as you remember these key points:

- **Find an agent that specializes in burial insurance.**
- **No trustworthy company will sign you up without an agent.**
- **Always get a second opinion if the cost of a policy seems too high.**
- **Read ALL the literature handed to you about plans.**
- **No matter your circumstances or condition, you DO qualify for a policy.**
- **Do your research before making any final decisions.**

You have nothing to fear. If you're in any way familiar with life insurance, final expenses should not be difficult to navigate, and if not, it is not hard to find resources or someone to help you. This article is an excellent jumping-off point to expand your knowledge and continue the process.

No one wants to worry or be consumed with the financial costs that naturally occur when a loved one passes away. Therefore, burial insurance covers a wide range of face values and medical conditions/illnesses. It provides extra coverage for the funds to pay off remaining medical bills or debt or need available cash for funeral expenses; burial insurance guarantees that those left behind will provide the best memorial they can and mourn without unnecessary stress or hardship.

Funeral and Memorial Service: Why You Should Plan Your Own

Obviously, planning a funeral of your own is usually not a thing anyone can be excited about. Honestly, who will be?

However, did you know? Doing so is essential and highly valuable.

How about a ritual joke to cheer up before we get down to business?

I think I found a good one...

It surprised me a little when I received the receipt from the funeral home. At the bottom of the receipt, after the invoice, he said, "Thank you. Please come back."

Seriously though, if you're thinking of planning your own funeral ahead of time, we compliment you. It only takes the courageous to do that, and it's worth it.

In order to help you more on your quest, in this article, you will learn why you should plan your own funeral, how to go about it, and learn about four different ways to pay for the funeral.

Why You Should Plan Your Own Funeral

Why you should be planning your own funeral is quite simple.

If you are not planning your own funeral, your family will have to do it, and it will be in their saddest time.

Here is the hard truth for you.

After passing away, your family will have dark times, filled with pain and sorrow. They will miss your absence so much.

Planning your funeral would not only be a difficult choice for your friends and family, but they also experience emotional stress because of your passing.

We don't like to think about their mortality, much less plan it. It would be best if you took the time to do this for your family so that they do not have to go through the greatest emotional stress in their lives.

Here is Some Very Good News

Planning your own memorial is an effortless process; in fact, it will take less time than you would ever think it will before you get things done.

All you need to do is a precise documentation of how you want to be remembered.

The best thing about the planning is that you only get to do it once, and you might even forget you ever did.

If you can commit a little time planning this in advance, it will pay off immensely in the future.

Eventually, you will save your family the pain, emotional stress, and the money, and it will further show them how much you loved them because of what you did.

It Would Help if You Documented Your Plans, or They Are Not Worth It

Usually, you could use a piece of blank paper, and that would be enough.

Irrespective of how you do it, you need to document your final desires, or the whole preparation will be useless.

In addition, even though you might transcribe the funeral plan, you need to keep it in a place where your family could easily access them.

The idea is that when you pass away, your family will naturally find your ultimate wishes so that they can follow your instructions. This will make it easier for them not to make these difficult choices when they are sad.

In the end, how you document your wishes does not matter. All you have to do is do it so that your family can use it.

How You Can Plan Your Funeral

The process of planning your own funeral is a process you will be familiar with.

And I am very serious about this.

Think of the process this way.

If you own a vehicle or you have ever bought. You will understand this more.

Think back to your last car buying experience. The process must have been like this.

- You calculated the budget.
- Decide the type you want, whether a car, truck, van.
- You establish the brands and models you are interested in.
- Compare the models to find out which one you prefer.
- Select a model.
- Selected color, internal and external options.
- Finally, you bought the vehicle.

The process of planning your funeral is similar to the one above. The difference is you won't receive the item now, and you will be choosing funeral-related options instead of a car.

Burial, Cremation, or Donation

The biggest choice you will make is whether you want them to bury, cremate, or donate your body to science.

Your budget can play a role in deciding which one to choose.

Keep in mind that the cost of a funeral varies greatly between these three options. On average, a regular funeral service will cost between $ 7,000 and $ 10,000. In comparison, a cremation service will cost between $1,500 and $5,000. It usually won't cost you anything to donate your body to science.

With affordable funeral life insurance plans to cover final expenses, most people can take out insurance for an amount needed to cover any memorial they want.

What to do with the remains if you choose funeral or cremation

If you decide to be buried, you will need to choose what you want to do with the coffin. If you want to be cremated, you must choose where the urn or ashes will be placed.

Either you believe it or not; there are several options. Each has its pros and cons, so decide which one works best for you.

In the Ground for Burial

This is the general burial, so to say. The coffin will be placed inside a tomb that is about six feet underground.

In the Ground Lawn Crypt for a Burial

A lawn crypt is a prefabricated tomb usually made of concrete and steel, through which several caskets can be stacked on top of each other.

Lawn crypts are sometimes mentioned in the ground mausoleums as they are essentially a completely closed shell, which preserves the coffin much better than a buried vault.

Above Ground Lawn Crypt for A Burial

This is the same as an in-ground lawn crypt, but it's above ground. It allows for the proper water drainage to ensure the enclosed casket is preserved.

In a Private Mausoleum Above Ground for Burial or Cremation

The mausoleum is an overground structure built specifically to house the remains of one family. Private mausoleums are very expensive, but a private mausoleum is the best option if you want exclusivity and privacy for the whole family.

In a Public Mausoleum on Land for Burial or Cremation

Public mausoleums were built in many cemeteries. This means that anyone can choose to place their remains there. Normally, those who choose this feature simply do not want their remains to be placed underground.

The very essential thing that you should know about the community mausoleum is there is no privacy. Therefore, other people you did not know will be placed alongside with you.

Natural burial

In this case, there won't be an embalming fluid, casket, or burial vaults. Instead, the remains are buried directly in the ground, allowing the body to decompose naturally.

Sometimes, in natural burial, they use some biodegradable casket or shroud, as long as it doesn't prevent the debris from decomposing.

Green Funeral

This is almost like natural burial with a fundamental difference. To keep the burial green, the cemetery where the remains would be placed must not use any kind of pesticides, and no other bodies in the cemetery would be buried using embalming fluids or coffins.

Spreading Ash for Incineration

One of the commonest options for those who want to be cremated is to ask for their ashes to be spread in an important location.

Of course, spreading ashes is an option, but make sure you follow local and state laws. All states are different, so don't go with assumptions. In general, some states and local regulations allow this, and others do not. In addition, those who allow this generally have restrictions on where you can distribute the ash, so make sure to check before using this option.

Memorial Cremation Reef

The Memorial Reef is a special option through which the ashes of the body can be mixed with concrete, turned into a statue of an object (it can be any shape of your choice), and placed at the bottom of the ocean.

You will need to work with a company that provides these services. You don't want your family to do it alone.

Do You Want a Viewing or Not?

Do you want your relatives to have one last chance to visit your body? Some like it, some don't. The choice is definitely yours, but you have to decide what you want.

The viewing can happen at the funeral home, a church, a synagogue, or any other place of your choice (as long as the building owner agrees).

However, you have to know that if you prefer to donate your remains to science and you want people to view it, then you have to pay the cost.

Now Choose the Details to Complete Your Plans

At this stage, you must have chosen between burial, cremation, or donation. You have chosen what to do with the remains and decided whether you want people to view or not.

All you need to do now is complete details such as location, flowers, music, and other things you want.

Check out the list below and decide which one is right for you. Then document what you want along with everything else.

- Location of the memorial service

- Where the remains will be place

- Attendees

- Type of casket

- Flowers

- Music

- Open or closed casket for a service

- Marker/headstone preferences

- Clothes, glasses, and jewelry to be worn for a viewing or final resting.

- Obituary preferences (key points you want to be addressed in your obituary)

- Any military preferences for veterans

- Name(s) of those who you want to make your arrangements.

- Post funeral reception preferences.

- Pallbearer suggestions

Four Ways to Pay for Your Funeral

At this point, you have fully planned your funeral, which means your family will not have to make these difficult decisions while mourning your loss.

Now, all you need to do is create a plan to keep your family from paying for the funeral costs.

Here's the deal.

The greatest burden you can place on your loved ones is to put the cost of your unpaid funeral on them.

In fact, most families don't have the money needed to pay for the funeral in full. As a result, a loved one will end up taking loans to ensure you have a respectable final funeral service. It often takes years to pay off the loan they took.

Even if you do not do anything, please ensure to prepare yourself financially for your funeral, so that your family does not have to borrow money to do it for you.

Now that you know, you have four simple options to pay for your funeral expenses.

AL KUSHNER

With that being said, you have four main options to cover your final costs.

Life insurance

Life insurance is a very popular option to pay for burial expenses, primarily because it offers immediate protection.

Also, there are life policies specifically designed to cover final costs. Usually, they are referred to as "funeral insurance for the elderly" or "final expense life insurance."

These are small policies designed to provide sufficient insurance to pay for burial expenses. These kinds of policies are very useful for people over 80 who are unlikely to qualify for a regular life insurance policy. The cost of a burial policy is usually affordable because the face amount is small.

Affordable Option

Only those who are financially disciplined should consider this option. Basically, you decide to set aside a certain amount each month until you have enough money to cover all your final expenses.

The obvious disadvantage of this option is that if you pass away without saving enough, your family will have to meet up with the remaining.

Pre-Need Agreement

This policy is a contract between you and a certain funeral home. You plan your funeral entirely with them, and they tell you the complete cost.

This policy is supported by one type of life insurance, but it is a different policy type than the one you get individually. The main difference between a pre-need policy and a single purchased policy is that the payment for a pre-need policy stops in one day.

The funeral homes that offer the pre-need police will try to make you pay the total cost within three to five years. Due to this, the monthly payment for the pre-policy payment can be expensive. They usually cost between $100 and $500 per month, depending on the total cost and the amount of time you give yourself to pay.

Inheritance Funds of the Deceased

While not recommended, you can be confident that your family will sell your home, investment, or other assets to cover your final expenses.

There is no doubt that this is an option.

For the most part, though, it should be off the table.

We are saying this because:

It takes a long time for your family to liquidate your property. First, the probate process can take months. Which is enough to condemn your family for a temporary attempt to raise money to pay for the funeral.

Even after they complete the probate process, they will still have to sell any valuables you have, which will take even longer.

Again, this is an option, but given the time it takes to do this, it should be the last option to be considered.

Having a Will or Living Trust

A living trust or will address legal issues related to your death, so it's important not to miss this step.

Now, whether you go with a living will or a trust is a personal choice and will probably be determined by the complexity of your property. This article provides a great resource of the pros and cons of each.

We suggest consulting with a will or trust lawyer and let them help you decide the one that suits you most.

If you're kind of independent, though, and want to create a will for yourself, that's fine. Sincerely, many people successfully set up a will on their own.

A lot of resources are available online to help you draft a will. If you are good with following instructions, then the process will be simple and accurate.

If you decide to draft a will without the help of a solicitor, use at least one guide to make sure you are doing it right.

On the other hand, a Trust is much more difficult and needs to be done with the help of a professional. From the application to structure, they are very different and are regulated by different laws; therefore, professional legal assistance is recommended.

You may be wondering ... Why you would need a will or trust?

It is very simple.

It would be best if you had a will or trust to strengthen legal issues related to death.

Like all other elements of your funeral, if you are not preparing for the legality, you are condemning your family to deal with them.

PRE-NEED VS BURIAL INSURANCE PLAN

There are many different options available for ensuring funeral payment when you or a loved one passes on, and it can be very overwhelming and stressful to decide what works for you. You've probably heard of preneed insurance plans but aren't exactly sure how they differ from burial insurance or final expense policies. Preneed, also called prepaid, plans are vastly different, and only advisable in certain situations.

In this article, we're going to discuss the advantages and disadvantages of prepaid insurance plans to help you decide if this method is best for your personal and financial needs.

What Exactly is a Prepaid Plan and What's Involved?

Prepaid plans are another way of ensuring your family is not burdened financially with final expenses after you pass on. Unlike burial insurance, prepaid plans do not have to be through an insurance company – usually you deal directly with a burial home or cemetery of your choosing. You and the funeral director create a contract with set arrangements, including flowers, music, casket, cemetery plot, embalming, transportation fees, gravesite, opening the ground, and all other burial services (cremation, etc.) to already be arranged before you or your family member passes on. The amount paid can either be in a lump sum or monthly payments. Depending on the plan you choose, monthly payments can range from $50 - $150.

So, When Is This Sort of Burial Expense Arrangement Advisable?

There are certain circumstances or situations in which this process can be best for you and your family. One advantage is the arrangements themselves will already all be taken care of when you pass away. This saves your family the emotional stress or burden of having to make all the arrangements themselves, which sometimes can be overwhelming and confusing. If you take care of everything with the funeral home or cemetery of your choosing beforehand, your family can mourn without further emotional distress.

These plans are also advertised to have your or your loved one remembered in exactly the fashion they choose. This is true – by making the arrangements yourself, you get to choose the plan or the details of how you want to be remembered in exactly the way you would like. This can also relieve your family of the emotional stress of having to choose details or services that they think you would like. If you are buried, they would have to pick the arrangements they think is best, or if you decide to be cremated, to choose where you would like your ashes placed, if you wanted them placed anywhere at all. Some people decide to keep the ashes of a loved one in their home, so it is as if they are still there with them. If you do not stipulate what precisely you would like beforehand, they would have to decide for themselves. This can be unnecessary stress, especially if the death was unexpected or accidental.

Prepaid can also be a good plan for you if there is a funeral home you are already familiar with and trust that costs will not increase, and they will honor the arrangement made. If you or your family member likes a particular place and has already decided what they want, this can be an easier offer than trying to find the right burial insurance policy. Payments could be taken care of immediately if the funds are available, and if not, it could be deducted monthly like a car or mortgage payment. There is no need to option different companies and find an agent as is required with final expense policies.

Prepaying your funeral can allow you to protect your Medicaid. If you know for sure you'll need Medicaid, you can get a Medicaid-exempt trust. Money in an irrevocable trust is excluded from your assets when you receive social security and/or Medicaid benefits. If you place your money in a revocable trust, it can be taken by Medicaid if your finances are otherwise drained.

However, if there is not a specific company, you're familiar with and know very well, there are many possible cons/dangers with pre-need plans that are usually not considered.

Funeral homes change owners, sometimes unexpectedly. You could feel safe with one owner, but if unforeseen circumstances occur, there's no way to guarantee how a new owner will handle your arrangements and possible monthly payments. Expenses could be added, or they could find faults in your contract asking for more money. This is not to say something like this will happen, but it is a possibility to acknowledge.

There is also a chance that funeral directors could declare bankruptcy. Instances like these are hardly foreseeable – there is no way to know if upon dying, costs will not increase, or if your payments can be refunded. There is no air-tight guarantee, so potentially you or your family could be out a large sum of money with no chance of getting it back. Again, this is not to say this will happen, but it is important to consider. Buying any sort of insurance or entering into any legal contract, particularly ones involving as much money as funeral expenses tend to be, should be met with much forethought and analysis. These companies are out to make a profit – so it pays to consider all alternatives and circumstances.

Another disadvantage to prepaid funeral plans is once you've decided, you can't change your mind. Say you or a loved one decides to be buried elsewhere – your money won't be returned from the company you've already committed to. This is true with any insurance policy as well, but prepaid plans are more finite. You have committed to a particular funeral home and a particular arrangement of burial; therefore, it is your final decision. No going back whatsoever. So, if you're unsure, or feel you might change your mind, please consider this factor. It can potentially be a very expensive decision.

Furthermore, there are no death benefits to leave behind for beneficiaries with prepaid plans. Should there be unexpected additional expenses, there isn't any extra money to draw from unless the family is in a financial position to take care of it. Since there is no way to forecast how much these costs could add up to, this leads to possible debt. Also, if you pass away before the plan is paid off, the remaining amount owed needs to be paid by the family. They can rearrange a new plan with the funeral director, so it doesn't need to be paid in full immediately, but if you don't want to possibly burden your family, this may not be the option for you.

Taking care of your final arrangements before you pass on is never a joyful activity, but it is necessary to ensure your family is taken care of and has the least amount of emotional and financial stress to handle after you pass on. Prepaid can be the right choice for you if you know there is a certain cemetery or funeral home you want to work with or if you already have the preparations you want for your burial or cremation in mind. Truthfully, however, only if you have the amount of money to pay outright is this an option you should consider. Burial insurance policies through an insurance company could possibly leave your family with a financial legacy or take care of other unexpected expenses. You always want to heavily weigh your options when making a choice.

What Exactly Is Modified Burial Insurance?

Final expense plans (also called **burial insurance, modified whole life insurance**, and **funeral insurance**) are issued through insurance companies specializing in that particular field. These plans are great if you need extra coverage, are looking to cover a funeral, and/or have been rejected by life insurance.

Burial insurance policies have underlying rules that no matter what policy or carrier you choose to go with, will always be true. **Prices, or premiums, will never increase, coverage will never decrease, cash value increases** that you can borrow from, and **policies will never expire.**

What's great about these particular policies is that the amount covered is given in a lump sum: a tax-free check to do with as you see fit. You can cover all final expenses and possibly any remaining hospital bills or debt if there is enough. It is possible you could leave a financial legacy to your chosen beneficiaries. This in and of itself is enough reason to choose a funeral insurance policy over prepaid plans; however, let's go through the details of acquiring a burial insurance plan and why they may be the better option for you.

Burial insurance plans are usually divided into three categories within companies:

- **Level benefit**

- **Graded**

- **Guaranteed issue**

*There is a fourth option called **modified** plans, which most insurance agencies will strongly advise you **against.** We will go into greater detail as to why later.

Level benefit plans are excellent if you do not have any complicated or severe health risks and are looking to cover burial expenses. These plans are essentially the best available, offering full coverage and benefits from day one at standard rates (the cheapest you can expect from any carrier).

Graded plans are available to you if you have health risks/conditions that are mostly controlled and not considered severe or high risk by a carrier. Usually, there's a two-year waiting period before full benefits with these plans, and the rates can be a little more expensive depending on the company. Coverage increases with each passing year until the two-year timeframe is met.

Guaranteed issue policies are for anyone with severe and/or multiple health risks that most insurance companies wouldn't be willing to accept. There is no underwriting process required; if you're able to sign a legal contract, you'll qualify for these plans. These policies have a two-year waiting period and cover a less percentage than graded plans. If the insured person passes away within the two years, the beneficiaries will receive a refund on their monthly premiums plus 10%. Accidental deaths are also covered from the moment you sign, which can be very important depending on what particular illness you may have.

Insurance companies usually have two factors they consider when deciding what kind of policy and premium you qualify for: **underwriting and prescription history.**

Medical underwriting is essentially a series of health questions that determine what conditions/illnesses you have and the possible seriousness and complications of said conditions. These questions range from simple questions like your height, weight, alcohol/tobacco usage, to more detailed queries like if you've ever been diagnosed with HIV or experienced an insulin shock.

An insurance company will also look at your **prescription history** to determine your policy. This is how the carrier validates your responses to the underwriting procedure. There is no extra work required on behalf of the insured; it's a quick process done electronically via your pharmacy.

Note: No medical exam or physical is ever required.

It is possible that if you have health risks or do not qualify for a level benefit or graded plan, you'll hear about **modified** plans. There are many reasons why most agencies will strongly urge you against these plans and deem them worthless. It's important to understand exactly what this plan is and why it's professionally inadvisable.

Modified plans, like graded and guarantee issue policies, have a two-three year waiting period; however, it'll only refund your payments plus interest. The amount of interest paid varies by company and your particular premiums, not the death benefit itself. This range of interest varies as low as 8% to as high as 30%, but most of the time the amount paid will be 10%. Say the insured person passes away during the waiting period before full benefits are granted, and the carrier pays the usual 10% interest. If $1000 was paid overall, the beneficiaries of the insured person would receive a tax-free check for $1100.

Normally this plan is offered to those with serious health risks because there's limited or no medical underwriting required, just like guarantee issue. However, these plans have premiums that can be incredibly expensive because the carrier doesn't know how much risk they're taking on. Modified plans and guarantee issue plans have many similarities, but guarantee issue, as we've stated, covers accidental death from day one. You could be paying the same amount but have at least some form of immediate coverage. With modified plans, you have no immediate coverage. When it comes to insurance, you want to get more bang for your buck, to put it bluntly, and a guarantee issue plan offers you more than a modified plan would.

What is more, even if you have a high-risk condition, you may be able to qualify for better than modified or guarantee issue plans. This is true for diverticulitis, cholesterol issues, blood clots, asthma, Crohn's disease, arterial fibrillation, bipolar disorder, type 1 diabetes, cancer (over two years ago), type 2 diabetes, heart attacks over one year ago, diabetic neuropathy, and many more. **The policy you end up with and the premiums you pay all depends on the agency you work with and the company you choose.**

With that being said, let's go through how to pick the right agency and company if you decide a burial insurance policy is right for you over a prepaid plan.

Most final expense companies will not speak directly with you – they'll require an agent to mediate the process. This stipulation works in your favor because an agent's sole job is to find the best and cheapest plan for you, no matter your circumstances or conditions. When selecting an insurance agent, they must specialize in burial insurance policy. This way, they will be familiar with the companies that would work with you even if you're what's considered 'higher risk.'

Never let an agent tell you there are no options available to you because it simply isn't true. The reason there are guarantee issue plans is because if your situation is considered dire or very high risk, you can still get coverage. The premiums are higher, yes, but you do have some benefits and a form of coverage. You could be on dialysis, on stage 5 kidney disease, or have recently been treated for cancer (conditions most companies wouldn't accept) and qualify for a great guarantee issue plan. Gerber Life and Sons of Norway are final expense companies well-known for its guarantee issue policies.

There are many options when deciding how to financially handle a funeral or cremation after you or a loved one passes on. For many people, a final expense insurance policy through an agency and carrier is the path to take. There are many insurance options no matter the circumstance that can offer you a form of coverage – remember, the beneficiaries receive a check to do with as they wish, so it could take care of any additional unexpected expenses. Always do your research before choosing, and make sure your agent is well-versed in the industry.

Top-Rated Guaranteed Issue Insurance Company

There are dozens of life insurance companies out there that offer these no health question policies. Here are just some to name a few:

There are many life insurers that offer you insurance policies without asking questions about your health. Below are some of the life insurance:

AIG

Americo

Colonial Penn

Gerber Life

Kemper

Mass mutual

Metlife

Mutual of Omaha

New York Life

Transamerica

Sons of Norway – Most affordable

United Home Life

Vantis Life

Many of these insurers have a normal waiting period of two years. However, there are some that have a waiting period of three years. Apart from the different waiting periods of two or three years, the other significant difference is the premium charged by them.

So, which insurer is the best and the most affordable?

We highly recommend Sons of Norway, as it is the insurer with the most affordable cost with which you can also have an agent. You would not find them in every state. Another one is Gerber Life. Also, there is Mutual of Omaha, but they are sold directly to the consumer.

This means that if you don't have an agent to help you in the future. If you don't want to work with a funeral insurance agent for the rest of your life when you have other insurance needs, then contact Mutual of Omaha.

But, if you understand and appreciate the importance of working with insurance professionals who will always strive to give you the best, then you can work with us to buy the Sons of Norway policy. Like some of our past clients, you will probably need life insurance anytime in the future. You might be the one in need of it, a family member or a friend. Don't you think it would be best to have a nice burial insurance advocate working for you instead of looking for one yourself? Here are some examples of the rates from Sons of Norway.

Guaranteed Acceptance Burial Insurance for Sons of Norway

Female

AGE	$5,000	$10,000	$15,000	$20,000
50	$13.81	$27.63	$41.44	$55.25
55	$16.98	$33.96	$50.94	$67.92

60	$20.54	$41.07	$61.61	$82.14
65	$24.67	$49.33	$74.00	$98.67
70	$31.66	$63.33	$94.99	$126.65
75	$41.55	$83.10	$124.64	$166.19
80	$53.33	$106.67	$160.00	$213.33

Male

AGE	$5,000	$10,000	$15,000	$20,000
50	$18.30	$36.59	$54.89	$73.19
55	$23.41	$46.83	$70.24	$93.65
60	$29.04	$58.09	$87.13	$116.18
65	$35.41	$70.82	$106.23	$141.64
70	$45.29	$90.58	$135.88	$181.17
75	$57.63	$115.25	$172.88	$230.50
80	$69.93	$139.85	$209.78	$279.70

Super Simple Guide to Getting Burial Insurance for Your Parents

Five main funeral insurance questions asked fall under:

- Is It possible I purchase insurance for my parents' funeral?

- How can I purchase life insurance for my parents?

- How does taking out life insurance policies for someone else work?

- Do my Parents have to know I got them a life insurance policy?

- Am I able to purchase burial insurance on my parents?

The questions above are generally the most often asked. In some cases, it can be stress-inducing when you have parents that are seniors without a burial insurance policy set in place. As long as your senior parents are aware and you have an insurable interest, it's highly likely you'd be able to purchase an insurance policy for their funeral.

Is It Achievable to Buy Life Insurance Policies for Family Members?

Looking to purchase a funeral insurance policy for your senior parents? This question is asked daily and consistently. In short, Yes. Here we strive in providing stellar service and teaching you how to best cover the funeral expenditures for your parents. Furthermore, our step-by-step process is seamless on how you can proceed to purchase the burial insurance you need for your senior living parents.

Can I Purchase Insurance Policies for Other People?

Is it achievable to have a funeral policy for someone else? Yes, it's possible to buy funeral planning for others inside your family. The only exception to the rule is, the other person has to be aware of this.

Examples can vary from your mother or father, or closely related peoples, and even someone who has no family left and you simply falling under the next chain of kin. Simply provide the best result, peace of mind for everyone involved.

Would You Be Able to Purchase Life Insurance Plans for Your Parents?

Burial coverage for Parents over the age of 75

Having to buy insurance policies for older parents is much more crucial than given thought. Regardless of funeral quotes for your father or mother or burial insurance policies set in place for your parents above the ages of 75. Obtaining an insurance policy for them or someone else is much more seamless than one would like to think.

Sitting out there are countless insurance companies that cover burial as a part of their plans. Even offering packages that include instant same day coverages with the burial plan. Shouldn't something be mentioned about the insurance policies that include no medical exams? As stated beforehand, no medical exams are required.

What about in the instance my family has more than one funeral policy in place? This is completely normal, and okay by every means! Reason being that most if not all policies have holes in them unable to cover certain expenditures for their burial process.

In some instances, family members would like to leave legacies behind or even trust funds and stocks for their children(s). This question is asked all too often as well, and we're here to help. We provide you with a seamless step by step guide on how to accomplish this.

Zero Examination Life Insurance Policies for Parental Guardians

What quantity of life insurance is provided without visiting a doctor for a physical? The amazing part of an instant same-day funeral insurance policy is there are zero exams involved in the process! A streamlined entire life insurance policy with zero medical examinations!

Of course, there will always be medical health concerns and questions as mentioned previously, although it stops there. Each carrier is unique in the guidelines they have set. Once you are qualified to proceed, we are more than happy to help establish a relationship to ensure you are cared for by our highly recommended A+ carriers.

This in mind it's achievable to provide a precise quote predetermined by simple health-related questions.

What the Process When Burial Insurance Is Bought for Parents?

Is the insurance for burials worth the expense? Insurance policies for burials (other names such as, final expenditure insurance or even funeral insurance) are types of life insurance policies that bring all parties involved a sense of comfort in the mind.

When it comes to comparing the difference between life insurance fees and funeral expenditures that accrue over time the two are far and wide. On the other hand, when it comes to policies for the final moments these can include coverages from medical billing, directors for the funeral, funeral housing, and countless other things.

In any case when it's time that your family member(s) pass a form for their claim will be completed and returned with their certificate of death. Throughout this process, we will stick by your side. We understand emotional times like these can be difficult, so we are here for you.

Purchasing Insurance Policies for Parents Funeral

Am I able to acquire insurance for the burial of my parents? (otherwise known as final funeral insurance for guardians)

Let's face it, your parents resolved all your problems maturing into adulthood. In this scenario, circumstances change and now you're the adult asking if it's possible to purchase insurance policies for your parents' funeral?

This type of insurance for their burial is simply the most advisable thing to do for you and your family. Things to have on hand when calling in for quotes:

- **Weight/ and Height**

- **Current Mailing Address and Valid Phone Number**

- **Previous Medical History with Prescriptions (Current and past changes with medication)**

- **History anything Medically Involved (Surgeries or even Procedures done)**

- **Health Condition**

- **Who is the one buying the policy? (Who pays the insurance premium?)**

- **Beneficiary Name(s) (Include Birthday)**

- **Coverage amount wanted.**

Key Distinctions Between Burial Policies and Life Insurance Plans for Parents

Aren't Life Insurance Policies and Funeral Insurance Equivalent?

What are the differences between the two policies for life and burial insurance?

Insurance for Burials What is this?

In short, this is a form of life insurance. Yes, they are equivalent to the things they do. Insurance for burials is nothing beyond whole life insurance plans made easy. Let's relay back to the question - is it possible to purchase life insurance policies for my family members or parents?

To be clear the term life insurance is often described as the most common kind of insurance for your life. This typically being purchased at younger ages in life. These policies render from 10, 20, or even 30-year terms for their policies. Typically backed by a medical examination for the asking coverage.

- Terms that have all equivalent value in meaning

- Final expenditure insurance

- Insurance for Burying family

- Crematory process insurance

- Insurance for Funeral

The process to buy an insurance policy for your parents' burial is beyond a seamless process to have happened. With today's technology, this can easily be done in less than 30 minutes to activate yourself a policy. Take it easy now as with the coverage you purchase will now cover your final expenditures as everything is part of the same plan.

How do I know if my policy contains a cash value? Over a length of the time yes, these burial policies do gain monetary value. When the time does come contact the insurance agent you are working with and they should be able to provide clear illustrations on how this process works.

What Do I have to Know About the Goodman Triangle?

IMPORTANT: Tax Knowledge that will save you! Give us thanks later!

If you take anything away from this, understanding that there are three major components in the Goodman Triangle will take you miles ahead in the understanding of the burial or life insurance policies available.

In examples such as this, if the person being insured (PARENT) is a different person than the individual paying (YOU) and in the instance, the beneficiary is someone related to you, perhaps a brother (JACOB) in the event your guardian dies, JACOB is the person who will claim the death benefits as in this instance is the beneficiary. Although as YOU are the person paying for this, in the IRS's eyes they will see this as a present to JACOB and of course tax you as they see fit.

Is it Possible to Avoid the Goodman Triangle?

Yes, to accomplish this - the people in the positions of the beneficiary and payor need to be the same.

What Coverage Is Given to My Parents for Burial Insurance?

Being able to reach serene states of living.

Typically, this is something that sits on the to-do list for a long time. Check that task off! Finally, you've set in stone a burial insurance plan that covers your parents.

Financial worries and this burden of figuring out what will happen after they leave has been lifted off of you, your mother, and your father. In any case, parents probably wouldn't feel so happy if they knew this was a financial burden that you had to carry that stressed you out.

Do I have To Tell My Parents I Bought Them a Funeral Insurance Policy?

Common Questions for Burial Expense Insurance for Parents

What information should I be aware of about funeral insurance policies for guardians? In most cases it's okay to feel overwhelming senses and have countless questions like the following:

Is it Required My Parents Take a Medical Examination? Life Insurance for Parents' Burials Does Not Require a Medical Exam!

No, unlike other life insurance policies out there, this kind is a simplified plan that includes Entire Life Insurance for Burials. APPROVALS INSTANTLY THE SAME DAY. If you have any questions be sure to ask your agent about them or other questions such as the terminal illness rider. This is typically built right into most insurance policies that cover burials. Companies that do this include but aren't limited to, Mutual of Omaha.

Is It Possible to Obtain a Quote or Rate for Funeral Insurance Policies and Plans Today?

How do I go about purchasing burial insurance for my guardians? In any instance to begin the process you can simply fill out the form on this page to the side or call us directly. We're here working for you as your independent agency sidekick. Available 7 days out of the week answering any questions that you may have.

Our Funeral Insurance Policies for Senior Living the Same as The Burial Insurance Plans?

Yes, as mentioned before the burial insurance name varies from person to person on what they need to be accomplished in their plan. Burial insurance policies typically remain similar in many fashions, although from person to person may be called something different.

What Happens If Health Issues Are Occurring With my Parents? What Burial Insurance Plan Works Best for Their Situation?

This depends on the health conditions your parents are in. The insurance type could vary and be graded differently to benefit in different ways that others couldn't. Although this in mind, they still qualify for immediate approval. Quotes for Burial insurance policies are generally based on eligibility. The way this is determined revolves around health-related questions and some underwriting inquires. Once data has been collected, we work within our partner program to provide the best accurate insurance rates for your funeral based on the information provided.

Is it Possible to Purchase A Funeral Insurance Policy if My Parents Live in A Different Location than I do?

This depends, it is highly advisable to work closely with your agent as from state to state there are regulated laws for instances such as purchasing insurance policies for burials. Modern technology will make it easy for you to figure out if you can or cannot. If you're living in Arizona and your Parents are in New York. The requirements for most insurance policies only require an over the phone voice signature or signatures via email for almost instant approvals in most cases. So, in most situations, all that is required to get started would be a mobile device.

Is it Mandatory I Get Consent from My Parents?

Can I buy an Insurance policy to cover the burial for my parents without their knowledge? In most if not all situations, obtaining life insurance policies on anything without consent will be labeled as insurance fraud. Along with this, you will need some form of insurable interest. Resulting in some financial burdens when guardians pass.

The Factors that Decide What's Included in Your Insurance Package

How much does it cost to afford a funeral insurance policy? Factors that can decide the monthly rate. Client age, current health conditions, do they use tobacco? Is there some form of congestive heart conditions causing the failure, or even including but not limited to COPD, etc.

Am I Allowed to Purchase More Than One Funeral Insurance Policy?

Will I get into legal trouble if I acquire more than one funeral insurance policy? The Truth is No! It is completely legal to have more than one burial policy in place. Commonly, people feel their policies do not cover everything that they'd like for the final expenditures. Leaving people not wanting their family to spend any money at all when they leave. In turn, requiring them to obtain other insurance policies to cover this.

It's very common that in most cases to have a preset life insurance policy and then when the time comes to purchase the burial insurance policy in place to ensure that the legacy and items are left to the next of kin in the family.

Am I Authorized to Pay for My Fathers Burial Insurance Policy?

Absolutely, yes. Your father's insurance will be covered if someone is paying the fee. This includes you being the payee and your father being the receiver of the insurance.

Of course, as mentioned previously insurance policies for burials differ from state to state, so this question would be perfect for your insurance agent working with you. For example, the product coverages and limitations from New York with different tremendously from another state such as Arizona.

What Is the Average Pricing to Put together a Funeral for My Guardians?

The most asked questions are how much do burial insurance policies cost? Generally, when it comes to the rate of a funeral across the country it costs around $8,000 upwards to $12,000.

Bearing this knowledge in mind, we've created a list of expenditures to be aware of when it comes to funeral services. Cremation on the other hand of course will tremendously reduce the price in expenses for a funeral and even these changes from location to location.

- **Funeral Casket**

- **Bouquets**

- **Directors fee for the funeral**

- **Transporting Casket & everyone attending a funeral (limo/ hearse)**

- **Funeral Ceremony**

- **Grave location and gravesite**

- **embalming**

- **etc...**

This kind of insurance covers all those extra financial expenditures that you otherwise would have to face when your guardians pass.

In instances where the guardian dies, the insurance company you're working with will send the beneficiary the benefits from the death. This in short will and should help cover all the extra fees accumulated for the process, including medical bills, debt, funeral fees, etc.

How Do Funeral Insurance Policies Work For Guardians Above Age of 50?

Is it allowed that I obtain a life insurance policy for my mother? Yes. In this example, let's say she's above the age of 50 and still healthy. Yet again, Yes. Her rates for this kind of insurance will likely be lower than normal.

Chances are your guardians have been putting this process off for some time. They'll likely be so happy you're assisting them with this process.

Burial Insurance Policy No Health Inquires for Guardians

For Senior parents experiencing higher-risk health conditions what are the best options for funeral insurance policies? When it comes to our loved ones who suffer from chronic illnesses, some companies do offer policies that contain guarantees. Similarly, they're not far in between traditional life insurance.

Of course, with exceptions such as the no health questions asked. Within this policy, the amount for coverages depends on the age limit which falls between 50 and 85 years young.

Burial Protection for Guardians More than 60

How would I go about getting a burial insurance policy set up for my Parents over 60?

Typically, around this time, your parents are still in well health.

Do you think this would be enough to pay for a burial?

Everything in mind, the answer simply would-be NO.

For many reasons, this is why so many families are turning and taking burial policies out on themselves including their guardians.

Consider this, are you sitting on $10,000 -$15,000 to expend for a ginormous burial bill?

Term Life Strategy for Your Guardian Funeral Costs

Is this something to consider?

No! Not even a chance! Let me explain why.

When Term Life Policies are considerable:

- Loan for a car

- Mortgage for a home

If you do need these covered for your parents who are over the age of 60. Then it is considerable to shop around for life insurance.

Along with this, a term length isn't such a bad idea to cover taxes on the estate. Also consider that at this age, 30-year length terms are no longer accessible to you. In the instance you need larger face amounts for longer lengths of time as seniority, consider asking us about our amazing GUL product.

Notwithstanding, to the extent to term.......

So, consider this when looking at the term, when the term terminates, of course, your parents will have aged, and consequently their health has had changes. This in mind your life insurance prices will dramatically increase.

This then forces you to weigh out your options about life insurance policies that contain guarantees and have no health questions. Paired with this is a two-year-long duration of waiting if your well-being has changed for the worse.

Policies of This Nature Cover Accidental Fatalities from the Beginning!

In most cases, your life insurance rate will rise a little.

(Keep this in mind, anything beats having nothing) ~ Is there $8,000 - $12,000 laying around your house for funeral expenses?

Once the decision is made for the insurance plan for your guardians, then comes the discussion of face amount and quotes for life insurance.

It's needed that you purchase a burial insurance policy for your guardians today, better sooner than later, and end up forgetting.

As well, with the age in your parents increasing so do your premium expense.

We all like to think the time is infinite. Simply, this is not true.

Our wellbeing can change at any instant, a tumble or anything could change you. This of course starts to drain you financially and on every other level.

Final expense life insurance with no exam is such an easy decision!

Funeral Insurance Policies for Seniors Over the Age of 70 Do Exist!

Of course, at this age, it's ideal to have some form of final cost insurance plan in play. Obtaining life insurance for your parents at this age of 70 has been made much easier than you'd imagine.

There is a reason you're here. You simply would like to supply your Guardians serene states of mind as they simply would like to bog you down with finances related to funeral expenditures in cases of their passing.

Quotes for Life Insurance Made Simple for Parents

Burial Insurance: How Much Does This Cost?

Average pricing for burial insurance is simply profile-based.

Here are a few reasons:

- Age

- Medicine currently using

- Medicinal history

- Surgeries, etc.

The following are monthly quotes for a solid 60-year-old male, non-smoker. The face measure of $15,000. Level advantages.

Sentinel Security $63.13

Security National Life $63.54

Mutual of Omaha $ 64.04

Instructions to Put Life coverage On Your Guardians

Simply take the first step in making the decision to have the conversation. Simply there's no reason to have the burden of the expenses when they pass. Talk about medicines they are taking and the conditions they have. As mentioned previously you need permission in order to purchase these policies for them.

When you and your folks are on the same wavelength, call us. No one is denied insurance coverage!

When the night falls, you will have serene states of being.

PART 2

HEALTH CHALLENGES

THE REALITY OF BURIAL INSURANCE FOR THOSE WITH DIABETES

Burial insurance policies are a great possibility for those who want a permanent policy for their final expenses, extra coverage, or have been rejected from life insurance. Payments from these companies are tax-free and are given a lump sum, so it can be very convenient if the insured person wants to make sure money will be readily available for their beneficiaries after passing away.

There are many stories of diabetics who have found securing a final expense policy either entirely impossible or inordinately expensive. This does not mean that as a diabetic you are at a large disadvantage for securing a burial insurance plan, or even an **affordable** plan. Those who experienced such difficulties finding burial insurance with diabetes worked with the wrong people or companies that did not have enough experience with their particular situation. Diabetes is now a relatively common condition; there are carriers that will be willing to work with you and offer better options than you would expect.

Securing a (in most cases, affordable) burial insurance policy is absolutely possible, no matter what type of diabetes you have or any condition you may have subsequently incurred because of it. Though every insurer has its own guidelines that control their plans, there are companies that will work with you even if your diabetes is not entirely under control. This applies to children looking to find final expense insurance for their parents as well.

In this article, we are going to go through why insurers care about diabetes, the plans that are available to you, complications related to diabetes and how insurers respond, finding an agent that is right for you, and how to secure the plan that best suits your personal and financial needs. Consider this article your complete guide to obtaining the final expense policy that's right for you.

The policy and rates offered to you by a carrier entirely depends on the type of diabetes you have, how controlled it is, and if you have any other complications or risks associated with your condition. Policy benefits range from $5,000-$50,000 depending on where you live and what company you choose.

Let's go over the overarching categories plans are sorted into, so you will know what they mean when mentioned later on. Practically every insurance company sorts their policies into the following three divisions:

- **Level benefit (also called Simplified)**

- **Graded**

- **Guaranteed Issue**

*There is a fourth category called the **Modified Plan** that can be offered to high-risk clients.

Most agencies will tell you to avoid these at all costs. The premiums are exponentially higher (anywhere from 40%-80% more per month) while still requiring a two-year waiting period. Should the insured person pass during that time frame, only the premiums paid plus 10% is offered back to you. Stay away.

Level benefit plans are essentially the best you can get. They offer full benefit and full coverage with standard rates (which are the lowest) from day one – no waiting period necessary. This may be an option for you if your diabetes is well under control and you do not have any other health risks.

Graded policies are the next best option of policy available. Even though there is a two-year waiting period, partial coverage is available and increases with each year. For instance, should the insured person pass away within the first year, beneficiaries could get anywhere from 30%-60%, and should it occur within the second year, the amount escalates to 70%-80%. Accidental deaths are also covered from day one – no questions asked.

Guarantee issue plans are for high-risk clients that companies may not want to take on. These are no questions asked policies that offer acceptance to anyone. Like graded plans, there is a two-year waiting period before full coverage. Should the insured person pass during that time, you will be refunded your premium plus 10%. These plans are often the most expensive because the company doesn't know what risks it is taking on and needs to compensate, but they are an absolute lifesaver for those with complicated situations. These may sound similar to modified plans, but they offer more for the higher costs than modified plans do. Guarantee issue policies cover accidental deaths from day one – modified plans do not. There is no reason to pay the most expensive premium costs while enduring a waiting period without receiving any immediate coverage at all. Plus, as we have previously stated, guarantee issue plans do not have any prescreening qualifications or questions before acceptance. If you are able to enter into a legally binding contract, you will be accepted. It really is as simple as that.

Why Do Insurers Care So Much About Whether or Not You are Diabetic?

The answer to why insurers care is relatively simple. Carriers want to know if you have been diagnosed with diabetes because of the serious complications that can arise if your insulin levels are not properly controlled. Diabetes is a well-known risk factor for cardiovascular diseases such as stroke, coronary artery disease, and heart disease. High glucose levels can affect practically every organ in your body, so either you are already a high-risk applicant, or you potentially could be one while you are on their policy.

Responses to your diabetic condition depend heavily on the type of diabetes you have type 2, type 1, or gestational.

If you have type 2, also called adult-onset diabetes, you are usually viewed as a lower risk for companies because your insulin can be easily controlled through medication and lifestyle changes. This could change if you develop complications, which we'll dissect in depth later on.

If you have been diagnosed with **type 1**, your options may be more limited because you are insulin dependent. This categorizes you as someone with a pre-existing condition. Complications can arise unexpectedly and be harder to control, placing you as a higher risk applicant. There are still many companies that accept type 1 diabetes, and we will go over that further in the article.

Gestational diabetes, occurring in some pregnant women who do not have diabetic symptoms before pregnancy, is not usually a concern. This situation is oftentimes temporary, as hormonal changes that happen during pregnancy can make a woman less responsive to insulin resulting in higher glucose levels. Often, this will essentially right itself once the woman is no longer pregnant, but sometimes it can continue after pregnancy, becoming type 2 diabetes. As stated previously, this is not something companies are overly cautious about and you could still have a fairly good chance at getting a level policy.

What do carriers require in order to place you with a policy? There are two main components to an application that determine if you qualify for a particular plan and what your costs could be: underwriting and prescription history.

The first, and most important, prerequisite is what is called an underwriting process.

Medical underwriting is required for all plans (except guaranteed issue). It is essentially a detailed series of health questions that companies ask to determine your risk factor, which in turn decides the policy they are willing to sign you on and if your monthly premiums will be standard pricing or higher. These descriptors range from very basic questions, such as height, weight, tobacco and/or alcohol use, to more specific queries like if you have ever been in a diabetic coma and how many units of insulin you take per day. Though every company has their own underwriting procedure, there are similar things, or red flags, they will all be on the alert for. The more detailed the medical question, the more attention they will pay to how you respond.

Note: No matter what, a medical examination or physical will never be required in the process of applying for funeral insurance.

Before anything, they will want to know how many health complications you have besides diabetes. The more conditions you are diagnosed as having, the riskier an applicant you are. Let's quickly walk through an example of the non-diabetic related risks they will want to know about. Expect to see questions like:

1. Are you currently confined to a wheelchair or using oxygen to assist in breathing?

2. Are you in a nursing facility or receiving Hospice Care?

3. Have you ever been diagnosed with AIDS, AIDS Related Complex, or any other immune deficiency disease?

4. Have you been diagnosed with Dementia, Alzheimer's Disease, or any other mental incapacity?

5. Within the past 18 months have you had the following...
a stroke, aneurysm, circulatory surgery, cardiomyopathy, heart attack, or heart surgery?

6. Within the past two years, have you been treated for or been diagnosed with internal cancer, leukemia, melanoma, liver disease, systemic lupus, or cirrhosis?

7. Within the past 18 months, have you been recommended to receive counseling or treatment for drug or alcohol abuse?

8. Within the past two years have you been diagnosed or treated for emphysema, tuberculosis, chronic obstructive pulmonary disease, or a Neuromuscular disease (such as Multiple Sclerosis, Epilepsy, Parkinson's, or Lou Gehrig's Disease)?

Note the time frames mentioned in certain circumstances.

These are conditions that could greatly affect the number of companies willing to accept you and the policies in which you may qualify. If you have any of the issues mentioned above, along with diabetes, depending on how severe the situation is, the best you would be offered is a graded plan. Guarantee **issue** is also always available to you. Please call an agent who specializes in burial insurance to talk with them about your options. You will have to pay higher premiums, but an agent can help find you the cheapest of your available choices. We will talk about finding the right agent for you later on in the article.

Now, let's move on to the questions you can expect to see concerning conditions that ARE connected to diabetes. Expect to see detailed queries asking:

- If you were diagnosed before age 50

- What medications you take

- If you've ever had a diabetic amputation

- Whether you've experienced insulin shock

- How many units of insulin you take per day?

- If you have neuropathy

- If you have retinopathy

- If you have been diagnosed with nephropathy

In very rare cases, you could also be asked about your particular AIC levels, any relevant family history, or the number of years you have been diagnosed as diabetic.

Notice there is not a question specifically asking what type of diabetes you have. This is because normally, companies will not come right out and ask whether you are type 1 or type 2. For whatever reason, they prefer to determine if you are type 1 or type 2 by posing questions that will reveal it. For instance, they could ask at what age you started needing insulin. Depending on your answer, (i.e., the younger you were) it could tip them off immediately that you are a type 1 diabetic. Companies will have their own age limits they set, so in some cases, your response could be enough reason to immediately reject you or you could fall within it. The policy you end up with depends very heavily on the particular carrier you are working with. As we have stated, type 1 is considered higher risk than type 2, so let's discuss what options you have if you have type 1 diabetes (as long as you are not diagnosed with any other flagged high-risk conditions).

Yes, it is possible many companies will reject you – but not all of them will. You could be charged a little more and have a waiting period (graded and guarantee issue plans) OR you might find a carrier that is perfectly fine with type 1. A good way to tell how a company might react is if there is an age requirement regarding insulin on the questionnaire. If there is not, then the company does not care, and your chances of qualifying for a level benefit plan skyrocket. Therefore, if you are type 1 diabetic with no other serious condition, you have a very good chance at finding an affordable plan that offers you a considerable amount of coverage – it all depends on the company.

The second factor insurance companies consider when determining whether or not to accept applicants and decide their policies is your prescription history. This process does not require any extra work or phone calls from you; the company analyzes your history electronically for you directly from your pharmacy. Companies do this because it is an effective way to validate your underwriting responses from a credible source.

Keep in mind certain medications solidify or tip-off carriers as to whether you have any more serious diabetes-related conditions. For example, if you are taking or have taken Humalog, Apidra, Humulin, Symlin, Novolin, Tresiba, Lantus, Levemir, Afrezza, Novolog, or Flexpen, they will coordinate the medication with the date you started taking insulin to determine not only if you have type 1 diabetes, but how under control it seems to be.

Another example is if they see medications in your history such as Calcijex, Eliphos, Omontys, Rocaltrol, Calcitriol, Sensipar, Carnitor, Zemplar, Fosrenol, Hectoral, Cystagon, Renvela, Levocarnitine, Phoslo, Renagel, Aranesp, or calcium acetate, they would be able to confirm along with your answers that you are or recently have been diagnosed with chronic kidney disease.

About 99% of insurance companies have their own set of risk classifications for final expenses. These are defined by preferred plus, preferred, standard, substandard. The riskier the rating, the more likely the policy comes with a waiting period and higher premiums. Very rarely will you have a waiting period that is more than two years. Since complications or conditions connected to diabetes will most likely place you in a higher risk category with a carrier, it is very possible you will have to wait the two-year time frame before full coverage no matter your complication.

Some of the conditions connected to diabetes that carriers will pay specific attention to or have certain limits and rules regarding include, but are not limited to:

- **Neuropathy**

- **Nephropathy**

- **Retinopathy**

- **Diabetic coma**

- **Insulin shock**

- **Taking more than 50 units of insulin a day**

- **An amputation related to diabetes.**

- **Chronic kidney disease**

Don't worry, we will go through each one so you can see what your options are, starting with neuropathy.

Diabetic neuropathy: About 50% of the people are affected by this condition that could be disabling. the most important risk factors to develop this condition, that damages the nerves, are smoking, obesity and high glucose levels on blood. The symptoms are related to the nerves that were affected. For example, if the nerves located on your feet are damaged, you will feel pain and numbness on that area.

Peripheral neuropathy is the most common type of neuropathy. This manifests in a tingling sensation or reduced feeling/numbness in your feet, legs, hands, or arms.

Mononeuropathy, also called focal neuropathy, is when you feel a sharp pain in specific facial nerves or in the middle of your body. Mostly common in older adults that do not have other long-term medical issues.

Autonomic neuropathy is a condition that affects the nervous system that controls internal organs like the heart, intestines, eyes, and stomach.

Radiculoplexus neuropathy, also called diabetic amyotrophy, proximal neuropathy, or femoral neuropathy is most common in those with type 2 diabetes and older adults. This form of neuropathy affects your hips, thighs, or buttocks. The pain normally ranges from severe to gradual weakness, meaning it might become more difficult to get up from sitting or even walk around.

Since neuropathy develops over time, many companies will outright reject you; however, there are select companies that are familiar with this condition and will work with you. Many times, you will be offered a plan with a higher payment rate along with a waiting period (graded and/or modified plans).

Guaranteed issue is always available to you – there are a couple of things you should expect if this is the road you follow. Just remember, payments will still be higher and there will still be a two-year waiting period. As we have discussed, accidental deaths would be covered from the day you sign. This is your best option if the person insured is very sick and needs coverage quickly.

Now, say you have nephropathy (kidney disease). This gets very specific. The most important aspect of this condition concerning what companies look at is the time frame. Often, this category will be split into two sections: your entire life, or within the last two years. If the only question they ask is whether you have had kidney issues within the last two years, and your nephropathy was over two years ago, you are good to go. The company will view you as they would a level benefit contestant with full coverage. Carriers that ask whether you have EVER had kidney issues will most likely require a higher premium or waiting period.

If you have had (or currently have) nephropathy within the last two years, the number of companies narrow considerably. You will have to pay more. Period. Whether or not there is also a waiting period depends on other health risks and what state you reside in. Plans are still available to you (remember guarantee issue), and there are even some immediate coverage options. An agent that is very experienced in dealing with nephropathy will help you find these options. Make sure they ask you specific questions about your nephropathy, such as what medications you take and if you have ever been on dialysis.

In essence, because nephropathy usually signals poorly managed diabetes, many carriers consider it high risk, especially if it is recent. You will have to pay a little more, but plans are available.

Let's move on to retinopathy, a condition caused by diabetes in which the blood vessels within the light-sensitive tissue in the back of the eyes are damaged. Retinopathy is more common in those who are insulin dependent. It can be a difficult condition to find coverage for if you don't have someone helping you who's experienced in this field. Just like nephropathy, the biggest aspect carriers consider is the time frame. Normally, there will be two categories, including if you currently have or had retinopathy within the last two years, or if your last experience was over two years ago. If you had it over two years ago, it will be like you never had it, so as long as you don't have other complicating health conditions, you will be placed in preferred or standard, resulting in a possible offer of a level benefit policy including standard rates and full coverage.

If you have had retinopathy more recently, meaning within the past twenty-four months, your options are more limited. Carriers will overwhelmingly want you to pay higher monthly costs and might impose a waiting period, i.e., a graded or modified plan. Modified plans come with both higher costs and a waiting period – remember, most agencies say to stay away from these kinds of plans. If you are not offered a graded plan, then guaranteed issue plans are always available to you. There are no medical questions asked before signing it.

Though pretty uncommon, sometimes blood sugar is too low or high, possibly resulting in a diabetic coma. No matter how long ago you had your coma or how many times, the fact that you had one at all will put you in a higher risk category with most insurance companies. How certain companies phrase their questions concerning diabetic comas are a good way of telling how specifically they will react and what they could offer you.

The three most common ways carriers will ask are if you have ever had a diabetic coma, if you had one within the last two years, or if it occurred over two years ago. The company asking if you have ever had a diabetic coma will probably reject you outright. If the company's question inquiries about the last two years and your answer is no, you will be viewed the same as someone who qualifies for a level benefit plan and standard rates.

If you have had your coma within two years, then your premium will be higher, and you might be imposed with a waiting period. Some companies may only want a little more money and offer you immediate coverage, though this is extremely rare. Graded or guarantee issue plans are what you can hope for, depending on the particular carrier's requirements concerning diabetic-related complications. It is up to your agent's expertise and what they can locate for you.

Ultimately, you will be charged higher premiums if you have had your coma within the last two years. Unfortunately, there is no way to get around that. The point is that policies are still available to you, and you can get coverage if you have experienced a diabetic coma.

Insulin shock occurs when there is an imbalance of insulin in your system, which relies on your food intake and exercise level. Failure to promptly respond to such an occurrence could result in a diabetic coma. As with the last diabetic complications discussed, the most important factor concerning insulin shocks is the time frame. If you had an insulin shock over two years ago and have no other concerning health conditions, you will be eligible for the level benefit plan, possibly without any restrictions (depending on the company).

However, say you experienced an insulin shock within the past two years. You will be charged a higher premium regardless of the company you choose. Very few carriers will only charge you more with immediate coverage – most likely you will also have a two-year waiting period. This leaves you with graded or guarantee issue plans. It is vital to have an agent who deals with diabetic clients often so they can find you the best companies to serve your interests and offer you affordable deals.

If you have needed an amputation as a result of your diabetes, a higher premium is inescapable because you will categorize for a carrier as standard or substandard. However, you will not necessarily have to endure a waiting period – that depends on what state you reside in and whether you have other health risks. Furthermore, though the cost is higher, it is still possible to find a policy relatively affordable.

There are certain plans where the increase is only around 10%, which is a very good deal given the severity of this diabetic complication. It is estimated that about 97% of carriers will decline a diabetic amputee, which is why an agent is imperative to obtain. Make sure the agent you choose asks comprehensive questions concerning your condition, such as when exactly the amputation occurred, if you are able to perform daily living activities by yourself, and if you are confined to a wheelchair because of said amputation. We will go over how to find the right agent for you later on in the article.

Time to tackle chronic kidney disease. You may also see this term referred to as renal disease – they mean the same thing. Every insurance company with an underwriting process will ask about kidney disease. This is a bit intricate because there are plans and stipulations for every stage of kidney disease. Because they need to know the stage you have currently progressed to, you will have to give your Glomerular Filtration Rate (GFR), which is the measurement of your kidney's level of function.

For reference, if your GFR is 90 or above, you are at Stage 1, if your GFR is between 60 and 89 you are at Stage 2, if your GFR is between 30 and 59 you are at Stage 3, and if your GFR is between 15-29 you are at Stage 4. There is a Stage 5 called End-stage Renal Disease, which means the GFR level of your kidneys is below 15. Along with your GFR, you will be asked if you've ever been treated for kidney disease – the type of treatment will also let the carrier know how severe and what stage you might be in. Dialysis, a kidney transplant, kidney failure (might be called renal failure) will indicate you're on stage 5.

Every possibility is open to you with chronic kidney disease unless you are in stage 5. You have to understand level benefit (simplified) probably will not be available to you unless your diagnosis is at the early stages, and with a healthy lifestyle and good management, you have a projected expanded life span. Bear in mind you will still have to pay higher premiums, but the advantage is you will secure full coverage and benefits from day one. Graded plans are probably the best plans you can hope to be offered, in which you will pay more, but will receive partial payment increasing with each year until full benefits are available (two years). Do not take a modified plan.

Let's talk about if you are at **Stage 5,** otherwise called End-Stage, Renal Disease. Kidney treatment is crucial, and you will most likely either have had a recent kidney transplant or you are soon going to need one. This places you in the substandard category for insurers, or the highest risk compartment. Therefore, immediate full insurance coverage is unfortunately not possible, and your chances of getting a graded plan are also very, very low. This is where guarantee issue plans come in and can be used to their full potential. Cases such as these, if this is your situation, are why guarantee plans are offered. Granted, they cost more, but you will still be partially covered. Your family will still have some help should you pass away within the two-year waiting span, and accidental death is covered from day one. There are several trustworthy and reputable carriers specializing in guarantee issue policies open to you. If you are able to sign a legal contract, you will be accepted.

Throughout the discussion of the most severe conditions connected to diabetes, it is doubtless you have noticed there has been a trend of needing an agent to find those certain companies that will accommodate and understand your certain circumstances and potential health risks. Especially if you additionally have other health conditions non-diabetes related, you are going to need an agent to find the best plan for your personal and financial needs. Most companies will not talk to you directly and will instead instruct you to find an agent in order to secure a policy. With that being said, let's discuss what to look for in an agent and how to know if they are the right one for you.

There are certain criteria you should look for in an agent whether you have diabetes or not, and certain factors they should especially possess if you do (ESPECIALLY if you happen to have additional illnesses/complications connected to your diabetes).

First and foremost, make sure your agent, or the agency they work for, represents at least ten different insurance companies. Ideally, these companies should rate as what is called 'top tier,' or the top in their field. These carriers could offer you more bang for your buck, essentially, and have already established themselves as reputable. An independent agency is best, as they have no specific ties to one particular carrier, and therefore will not push you in a certain direction because they will gain commission. The companies represented should be a wide variety; this way you will have the best chance at being offered a plan that works well for you. You never want an agent that is only familiar with carriers that offer graded plans, for instance. An agent or agency that is well versed in an assortment of companies is better suited to find a policy for whatever your specific requirements or circumstances may be.

Make sure your agent specializes in dealing with diabetic life insurance (burial insurance). It cannot be stressed enough how important it is to do this. Because every company deals with underwriting in their own way, an agent that is well versed in diabetic clients and pre-existing conditions, as well as the complications that may arise as a result, will know exactly how to handle it. A 'jack of all trades' agent might not be aware of all the possibilities and could pass you a plan that's far too expensive or completely unfit for you. They might encourage you to take a guarantee issue plan when another company would give you a graded plan. Take diabetic retinopathy, for instance. If you currently have retinopathy, there are only a select few carriers that will offer you immediate coverage.

An agent who does not regularly deal with diabetic insurance probably would not be aware of these distinct carriers, and you could be out immediate benefits while still paying higher prices. For another example, say you recently experienced a diabetic coma (within the last two years). An agent specializing in the field would find the companies that would still issue your coverage and should fight to find you the cheapest option available. Paying the least for the best is what your agent should do.

We have gone over very briefly what an agent should ask you in certain cases, but it is important to make sure you understand why they do so. Above all, whether an agent asks you specific questions about your condition is a good marker to tell if they are as experienced in burial insurance for people with diabetes as they should be. If you tell an agent you have diabetic neuropathy, and they don't ask you to detail practically everything about it – find someone else.

Agents need all the information they can get about your health, so they truly discover the best company and policy for you. Say you had neuropathy over two years ago. Remember, certain companies will ask in the underwriting process if you have EVER had neuropathy, or if you have had it in the past two years. Those who ask if you have ever had it will not accept you regardless of how you answer other questions. You want your agent to know what companies these are so they will not send you to a dead-end or stick you with a more expensive plan than is necessary.

It is vital to always be 100% honest when answering any medical questions your agent or carrier may require from you. Trying to hide a condition in fear that you may be charged higher premiums or have to endure a waiting period is not worth the risk. Insurance companies verify everything you tell them – the reason they check your prescription history (directly from your pharmacy itself) is for this very purpose.

Furthermore, if you have an agent who knows what they are doing and is very experienced in the field, they should be able to find you a policy that suits your needs no matter what you tell them. Even if you have a couple of complications from diabetes or risks separate from it, there are plans for you. It is not worth being caught later down the line by your company. At some point, you will probably need treatment for whatever the condition is you were playing down – your agent, or the carrier, might be notified. Not only might you be dropped from your plan, meaning you will be out all the money you paid so far, but the word could spread and your chances of being accepted anywhere else (that is not a guaranteed issue plan) could dwindle considerably.

With that being said, be careful that the company you go with is reputable and trustworthy. This may seem obvious – and we have already covered what an agent should possess and what to look out for – but there are a lot of websites posing as insurance companies that look impressive and credible when really, they are either just trying to take your money or trick you into additional fees. Therefore, it is worth discussing what to be aware of and how you can avoid insurance scams.

The most obvious way to tell if something is not what it seems is if the prices are too good to be true. Usually, you will see ads for companies or sites that boast the best prices on the market, and you will wonder how they can afford to keep their premiums so low. They can't – it is impossible. This means one of two things: either there will be lots of fine print detailing the extra fees you are incurring by signing up (for example, if you do not want a waiting period there will be an exurbanite charge to have immediate coverage – an option no reputable agency or company would offer you) or the entire site is a ploy to get your card information.

A good way to think about sites that option incredible prices then stick you with extra fees is a car salesman drawing up your contract when you buy a car. The price on the front windshield may look like an unbelievable offer, but when you finally sit down to hammer out the details, suddenly there are extra charges like financing charges for taking out a loan, registration and title fees, dealership fees, a security system, and any maintenance the car might require.

By the time you are done walking through the papers and contracts, you could end up paying far more than you would if you went through an agent and found a policy from a standard company. An insurance company is a for-profit business – so when you see too-good-to-be-true prices, that is absolutely the case. Every insurance company is going to make sure they make money off of you, that's just the unfortunate truth, so make sure the one you pick is one you trust and are truly happy with.

Sites with amazing offers that are purely fraudulent are normally only one or two pages, so double-check the rest of the site before inputting any financial information. If all you see is the page with the monetary offers and a space to sign up, it is not a real insurance company. Whoever is behind it will take your information and run with it, so be very careful.

Another tip is to never buy from a no-questions-asked TV ad or billboard. Again, chances are you will be burdened with multiple fees adding up to as much as you would be paying for a company that would offer you BETTER coverage and benefits. Something else to remember is that no credible company will talk to you without an agent; therefore, these sites claiming to be no-questions-asked while still asking for your credit card information should seem immediately dubious and untrustworthy.

By doing just a little research, you can avoid insurance scams and keep your money safe. Incidentally, never make a check or payment out to the agent – if yours asks for this they will probably pocket the money for themselves. Payments should always be made to the company directly; any dependable agent would know that.

Though you should always do research before making any choices, there are some companies and agencies with excellent reputations that also specialize in diabetic burial insurance that we can recommend so you have a place to start. Superior Mutual and Levinson & Associates are credible agencies deal with clients who have specific circumstances and might have more trouble finding a deal that is workable for them.

Sons of Norway is a reputable company well-versed with diabetics. They consider both type 1 and type 2 diabetics for people over the age of 50. If you have complications connected with diabetes, you may qualify for their guarantee issue plan.

Gerber Life Insurance Company is recommended on most agencies' websites because they have one of the best guarantee issue plans on the market. The minimum age to apply is 50 – consider this carrier if you have complications that would prevent you from securing immediate coverage from other plans and companies.

Prosperity Life Insurance Group does not have a minimum age for the onset of diabetes like Nassau does and is not concerned about the units of insulin a client is using per day. The age requirement for applying is 50 and over. They do not accept diabetic complications, however, so consider Gerber Life or Nassau if you fall under this category.

Royal Neighbors of America is another possibility for diabetics. There are stipulations though: you have to be over the age of 50 to apply, and you can't have been diagnosed with diabetes prior to 30 years old. But if you have diabetic complications this may be the agency for you. They do not care about the number of units of insulin you have per day and accept complications connected to diabetes. They have been reported to pay death benefits in a timely manner and offer competitive rates.

Sentinel Security Life considers type 1 and type 2 diabetes. You will not be considered for immediate coverage if you take over 50 units of insulin every day, but apart from that provision, they are a well-known carrier for diabetes and provide highly rated customer service.

Mutual of Omaha shows up on multiple 'best burial insurance providers' lists and accepts both type 1 and type 2 diabetics. The biggest condition, however, is you have to have been diagnosed for diabetes at the age of 50 or above. This disqualifies many type 1 diabetics.

Be cautious of carriers like AARP, Colonial Penn, and Globe Life that mail applications to you. The applications may not stipulate whether you have a waiting period or not before receiving full benefits. They may also try to pass of term life insurance plans as final expanse plans. These are not the same things – term life insurance plans expire, and you do not want to be 80 years old with no coverage. Furthermore, these plans increase their premiums after five years.

Burial insurance policies, once you choose one, should never increase premiums, no matter how much time has passed. This is how reputable plans work. Carefully read every piece of literature and contract (like disclosure agreements, etc.), handed to you by an agent or company to make sure you are truly signing on for what is being told to you.

There are many companies willing to work with diabetics, but the stipulations each company has is what your agent needs to help you with to find the best policy for you. Always get a second opinion if you feel you are being pressured into a policy that is not suitable for you or if it seems unreasonably expensive. Though there are reasons to do this process quickly, if you are afforded the luxury of taking your time, feel free to do so. This is okay. There is no need to rush if you don't need to.

Taking out an insurance policy of any kind is a big commitment, but burial insurance is a lifelong commitment. Should you cancel a policy, you will not receive any money back. If you then pick another policy with a waiting period, you will have to endure that time frame from the beginning all over again, so please be 100% sure before you choose your company and plan. Do not allow yourself to be forced by an impatient agent waiting to earn a commission. They do not have your best interests at heart.

All of this information is probably overwhelming and maybe a little intimidating, but don't worry. You only need to focus on the information pertinent to you and your agent will be a tremendous help to you the whole time. This is why we went over in intricate detail every aspect to be aware of and look for in a burial insurance agent. Once you have found a good one, the load on your plate becomes a considerable amount lighter. Just remember these key points:

- **Every type of diabetes can be covered.**

- **Timeframe is imperative with any diabetic complication.**

- **Track what questions the underwriting process includes regarding diabetes.**

- **There are some diabetic complications that are only available with higher premiums and/or a waiting period – no matter what.**

- **Find an agent specializing in final expenses for diabetics.**

- **Always be 100% honest with your agent and carrier.**

- **No matter your situation, there is a plan for you.**

- **Never make a final decision without doing the proper research**

- **Take your time.**

You are going to be just fine. There is no condition or situation you could have that would prevent you from getting a policy – guarantee issue plans exist for that very reason. There is always something available to you. Yes, the cost will be higher and there will be a waiting period, but truthfully, at the end of the day, it is better than no coverage at all. There are companies with very good guarantee issue plans if that is the choice you have to take.

All you need is the right agent to help you find the carriers that will work with you. It cannot be emphasized enough how important doing research is to this process, not only to make sure your agent is as good as they claim to be but to ensure the policy you have is truly the best one out there for you. Looking at customer reviews for both an agency and company, if you can find them, is perhaps the most effective method of ensuring you are with the right people.

With burial insurance, there is no such thing as a hopeless situation. This form of insurance was specifically designed to cover a very wide range of medical conditions/illnesses. Remember that, and do not settle for less than what you know you can have. Your expenses will be covered so your family is taken care of and looked after with less stress than is necessary.

Burial Insurance for Cancer Patients – A Complete Breakdown

To free our loved ones from financial burdens such as funeral costs, it is crucial to buy a burial insurance policy, notwithstanding how long cancer has been, knowing that burial insurance policy gives rest of mind and a more blissful life.

The Four Types of Burial Insurance Policies for Cancer Patients

Burial insurance quote differs for different life insurance companies, and they are four types of insurance policies available for all cancer patients. Therefore, it is vital to consult a burial insurance specialist to know your best option. The general policies for cancer patients are;

1. **Guaranteed Issue Burial Insurance Policy**: cancer patients with terminal and worst outlook are mostly offered the guaranteed issue policies. The guaranteed policies have the highest premium with two years period waiting for active coverage. If the cancer patients die of cancer during the waiting period, the patient's family will not get the insurance payout; they will only receive the interest on return and the premium. But if the cancer patients die from an accident during the waiting, the family will receive the full burial insurance package. Guaranteed burial policies have a limited death benefit. Cancer patients undergoing the following treatment: immunotherapy, radiation, surgery, chemotherapy, hormone therapy, and hormone therapy are

qualified for guaranteed issue burial insurance policy. A U.S citizen between the age of 50 and above can quickly get the guaranteed issue insurance policy.

2. **Modified Burial Insurance Policy**: the best option for a cancer patient that did not meet up to the conditions of getting a graded burial insurance policy is a revised burial insurance policy. Your beneficiaries get the insurance policy's full benefit if you pass away two years from the date the insurance was issued. They will also get close to 7/10 benefits of the insurance policy if you pass away during the second year of the insurance policy and only 3/10 benefits of the insurance policy if you pass away in the first year. Two years waiting period is inevitable for a cancer patient who has been receiving treatment for the past two years. It is an expensive premium for severe cancer patients.

3. **Graded Burial Insurance Policy**: graded policies have the lowest premium after level burial insurance policy with full insurance benefits and active coverage. They are for a cancer patient with good condition.

4. **Level Burial Insurance Policy**: The level burial insurance policy is better than others mention because it has the lowest premium. It is an instant active coverage for former cancer patients with no recurrence of cancer for the past two years. The level policy expects you to be in a good health condition before you can get the insurance. For this package, they are no medical test, only health questions. You get a fixed premium for the stipulated period and guaranteed death benefit that those not reduced.

Frequent Questions Asked by Burial Insurance Companies.

Suppose you want to apply for burial insurance policies for cancer patients. In that case, the burial insurance companies are likely to ask you some questions concerning the patient's full health condition and the treatment they have been receiving. In answering those questions, you need to be precise with all the information you gave them, so they don't reduce your benefit or deny your benefits. So, it is vital you know the nature of the questions they are likely to ask you, so you have the answers at hand.

The Nature of the Questions You Should be Expecting.

1. The type of cancer and its stage

2. The location and size of the cancer

3. Did cancer metastasize?

4. Do you have any family history of cancer?

5. When were you diagnosed?

6. Are you in remission now?

7. How long have you been in remission?

8. The type of treatment you have received and your treatment records.

9. Have you been diagnosed within the last two years?

10. Have you had cancer before? If yes, is it a different type of cancer or the same as the current one?

Cancer Patients that are Likely to be Turndown by the Burial Insurance Company or Pay a Higher Premium

1. A Cancer Patient with Multiple Occurrences of Cancer Diagnosis

Buying a burial insurance policy for a cancer patient with multiple cancer diagnosis occurrences is a no-go area because no burial insurance company will accept your application once they realize you have a multi cancer diagnosis or numerous cancer diagnoses.

2. A Cancer Patient with Metastasis Cancer

Due to the low survival rate of a cancer patient with metastasis cancer, burial insurance companies consider them as high risk. Therefore, most burial insurance companies are likely to reject your application. But it is still worth trying because some burial insurance companies may accept your application for a higher premium and low benefits.

3. A Current Cancer Patient

Burial insurance companies consider current cancer patients as high-risk customers. Getting a burial insurance policy for a current cancer patient will be difficult, depending on the carrier, knowing that they are different guidelines for different carriers.

4. Patient with a Malignant Brain Tumor.

Burial insurance companies will want to know if their clients have malignant because clients with such disease are of high risk. Burial insurance policy available for patients with a malignant brain tumor is modified or guaranteed a burial insurance policy. Note that not all benign brain tumors are cancer.

5. A Patient with Sarcoidosis.

Most burial insurance policy classifies sarcoidosis patients as cancer patients because severe sarcoidosis can be invasive and severe. It requires a biopsy to make a diagnosis. Sarcoidosis can affect many organs like the lungs and can get complicated. Most burial insurance companies will want to know if their clients suffer from sarcoidosis. Most burial insurance companies will want to know if their clients suffer from sarcoidosis. A patient with sarcoidosis will find it hard to an approved burial policy for a low rate.

Cancer Patients that are Likely to be Accepted by a Burial Insurance Company with Little Premium

A One-Time Cancer Patient (Someone That Once Had Cancer)

Applying for a burial insurance policy for someone who was once a cancer patient who is now free for the last two years gets an active coverage approval after an additional two-year minimum waiting period. Such patients get a level burial insurance policy with a low-rate stable premium for the policy period and full insurance benefits.

Acceptance of Burial Insurance Policies for Cancer Patients and the Premium

Accepting an application for a burial insurance policy for a cancer patient by burial insurance company differs depending on the cancer patient's condition (survival chance). The patient's cancer conditions also determine the premium. A Cancer patient with a low survival chance (such as melanoma) is likely to get turned down, short insurance benefits, and a higher premium. While a cancer patient with high survival chances such as squamous cell carcinoma and basal are likely to get their burial insurance accepted with the full insurance benefits and lower premium.

It is also essential to know that the cancer mortality rate differs with respect to gender and race. Men have a higher cancer mortality rate compared to women. Asian/Pacific Islander women have the lowest cancer mortality rate, while African American men have the highest cancer mortality rate.

Tips to Help You Answer Questions Asked by Burial Insurance Companies

1. Understand the status (type, stage) of cancer patients. i.e., go through the possible questions the insurance company is likely to ask you so that you can be in a better position to answer.

2. Consult an insurance expert.

Tips on How to Buy a Burial Insurance Policy for Cancer Patients

Can cancer patients purchase burial insurance? Of course, Yes! Although they are condition of two years waiting period attached to all burial insurance policy that is inevitable, dependent on the cancer status (the time you had cancer, the type of cancer, the stage if it has metastasis to other parts of the body, and so). It is quite stressful and costly to purchase burial insurance for cancer patients. Notwithstanding that present cancer patients only qualify for guaranteed issue life policy with smaller insurance coverage than other burial insurance policy coverage.

Check This Out!

There are various kinds of burial insurance coverage available for cancer patients who want to buy a burial insurance policy. And you would not be subjected to any medical test; you are only required to answer some health questions.

How Burial Insurance Companies Cover for Cancer.

They are various factors to put into consideration that will determine your expectation given your current cancer status. It is vital to know that different burial insurance companies have different coverage guidelines. Every burial insurance company is likely to ask about your health with regards to your cancer status.

Factors that Burial Insurance Companies will put to Considerations Concerning Cancer Patients

1. The number of times you've had cancer.

2. The last time you had cancer.

3. Your treatment records.

4. Type of cancer you have.

Those are the factors they put into consideration to determine the available burial insurance coverage for you.

Two Types of Cancer that Burial Insurance Companies Don't Pay Attention to

1. Squamous cell carcinoma.

2. Basal cell carcinoma.

Not all types of cancer are life-threatening; different cancer has a different mortality rate. Most burial insurance companies will clearly state their non-interest for such cancer. It is a no-go area for burial insurance companies.

Things You Should Know about Prescription Medications for Cancer and Cancer Treatments

They are some cancer treatment that burial insurance companies classify as cancer. To them, having such treatments is equivalent to being a cancer patient. Such treatments are:

1. Chemotherapy

2. Hormone therapy

3. Surgery

4. Immunotherapy

5. Radiation.

They are drugs prescribed for cancer patients; if you have had such a prescription, burial insurance companies will consider you a cancer patient. You should also be aware of the first fill protocol of most burial insurance company. It is their avenue to check when you first took certain drugs. If you have not been taking those drugs for at least two years, they won't consider you a cancer patient.

Some of the prescription drugs are:

- Abraxane

- Anastrozole

- Arimidex

- Aromasin

- Doxil

- Femara

- Methotrexate

- Novantrone

- Nolvadex

- tamoxifen

- Thiotepa

- Alkylating agents (cisplatin, chlorambucil, procarbazine, carmustine etc.)

- Antimetabolites (methotrexate, cytarabine, gemcitabine etc.)

- Anti-microtubule agents (vinblastine,paclitaxel etc.)

- Topoisomerase inhibitors (etoposide, doxorubicin etc.)

- Cytotoxic agents (bleomycin, mitomycin etc.)

Are You a Cancer Patient?

You should know that most burial insurance companies don't give coverage to cancer patients, and the few that do provide a two-year waiting condition. No burial insurance companies also provide instant coverage to cancer patients. The most beneficial burial insurance policy for a cancer patient is guaranteed issue burial insurance policy because it is a no health question policy. Not regarding the cost, guaranteed issue burial policy is a three ways benefit. Your beneficiaries get the burial insurance coverage after two years waiting period, if you pass away by accident during the waiting period, your beneficiaries will still get the full insurance coverage, and if you pass away within the two years waiting period, your beneficiaries will get the premiums you have paid with interest.

Questions Burial Insurance Companies ask Cancer Clients.

Burial insurance companies have different health questions, but their health questions are always structured in two-phase: Cancer at the modified division and cancer at the severe division. Once you apply for a burial insurance policy, you will have to answer some health questions. Let's talk about the two divisions.

Cancer at the Modified Division

1. Have you treated any internal cancer for the last two years?

2. Have you been counseled to visit chemotherapy for cancer in the past two years?

Cancer at the Severe

1. Are you presently a cancer patient?

2. Has it circulated over the other section of your body?

3. Have you had cancer more than once? If yes, is it of the same type or different type of cancer?

Knowing that burial insurance companies are different, those are the similar question they ask. You should know that the answer you provide them will determine if they will offer you coverage. Answer yes to all those questions means they will reject your application instantly.

What to Expect as a Cancer Patient?

You cannot get a burial insurance company that will ask for your cancer records for the past 1 year. As we have rightly said, all burial insurance company has a similar guideline policy of checking your cancer records for the past two years. Meaning if you've had cancer within the past two years, you will be subjected to some of their conditions (two years waiting period).

You Were Once a Cancer Patient in the Last Two Years.

Burial insurance companies consider cancer patients in this section as clients with the highest risk. Burial insurance companies that will give you coverage will be either a modified burial insurance policy or guaranteed burial insurance policy. Note that no matter the burial insurance policy they offer you, you can't skip a minimum waiting period of two years.

Modified Burial Insurance Policy: for a modified burial insurance policy, your beneficiaries will not receive the insurance coverage until after the two-year waiting period. If you should die within the two-year waiting period, they will only receive the premium you paid and interest. But if you pass away by accident, they will receive the full burial insurance coverage.

Guaranteed Burial Insurance Policy: few burial insurance companies that offer guaranteed burial insurance policy don't ask health questions or medical exams. The guaranteed burial insurance policy provides inferior insurance coverage compared to other burial insurance policies. It can cover only funeral and burial costs. Middle-age cancer patients, who want to secure their dependent academic fees, guaranteed burial insurance coverage small to cover such.

You Once Had Cancer Three Years Ago but Have Not Treated or Had Cancer for Two Years

Three years ago, you were once a cancer patient, but presently you have not had or treated cancer for the past two years. You are in a greater position to get a burial insurance policy with little cost and high and instant coverage because most burial insurance companies are mostly concerned with two years of your health status. Therefore, you can reply to their questions with no.

You've Not Treated or Had Cancer in the Past Three Years

Suppose you are in this division, better! Because no burial insurance company will reject your application since their cancer health questions are within two years. Therefore, you can select any burial insurance policy with the best burial insurance coverage and smaller premium, a level burial insurance policy.

Tips on How to Get the Most Beneficial Burial Insurance Policy for a Cancer Patient

They are many factors to consider in looking for the most beneficial burial insurance policy for a cancer patient.

1. It is safer and better to work with an independent burial insurance specialist.

2. No burial insurance company conforms to everyone's desire, so it is vital to visit as much a burial insurance company as possible.

Conclusion

Understanding the chances of your survival as a cancer patient will help you determine the cost of burial insurance policy and its benefits. The type and stage of cancer will also determine the type of burial insurance policy. Buying a burial insurance policy puts your loved ones and family in a better position for a future event.

A Complete Guide for Getting the Best Burial Insurance for Stroke Victims

Have you been considering buying funeral insurance, and you are worried that your stroke history will get in the way? If you already have a health problem, such as a stroke, it will cause the insurance company will pay more attention to you.

Do insurers classify stroke as a critical illness? Firstly, in order to make things clearer about how to get the best funeral or end-of-life insurance plan, either you or the person in question should prepare the following:

- Note the date when the last date was diagnosed.

- The type of stroke that was diagnosed; is it a mini-stroke called TIA – transient ischemic attack or the full-blown type, also called CVA – cerebrovascular accident.

- The medications you have been taken, and for how long?

- Any physical or mental ailments as a result of the stroke.

- Any other medical condition or disorder you and your family had prior to the stroke.

- Tobacco consumption history.

- Any past occurrence of stroke in the family.

Before anything else, these things, as mentioned above, will determine the type of funeral policy you or a loved one will be offered as a stroke patient.

Can You Qualify for Burial Insurance After A Stroke?

Yes, in fact, you can secure a low-cost burial insurance policy even if you have had a stroke.

First of all, helping stroke victims without insurance can be too unrealistic. In fact, some insurers will be more tolerant than others. We will deliver these carriers to you. In most cases, funeral insurance can be obtained for stroke victims, and yes, the coverage will start from day one. We have insurers who specialize in stroke, and they will offer you a level benefit, even if you were prescribed thinners the day before.

Many of our clients with stroke seem to have expressed similar concerns. Luckily, they found us, and we sorted things out for them. Today, we will take you through how you can also get a life insurance coverage.

You learn about the reaction of funeral insurance companies to an applicant who has had a stroke, the options available, and, most importantly, how to get the best plan.

Here is the Real Deal for Burial Insurance after a Stroke

You will not find one funeral insurance company that does not specifically ask about strokes. Please note that the full-blown is entirely different from the mini stroke (TIA). If you had a mini stroke, read this article. Mini strokes are not very serious and severe, and your options are much better than options if you had a full-blown stroke.

Here is the Bottom Line

In all sincerity, your options and how good it is will solely depend on when you had previous experience with stroke. It does not matter when there are better options available for you. If the stroke has occurred within a year, then you have to wait, and you will pay a slightly higher premium. At the same time, for more than a year, you will be entitled to the lowest rates with immediate coverage.

Here's Another Very Interesting Thing

Did you know there is no need to undergo a physical exam when you sign up for a final expense life insurance plan? Yes, you read that right. You will only answer questions about your health.

A stroke is a serious medical event, so it can greatly affect the cost of life insurance. Fortunately, we can help you get the best plan possible irrespective of the last date of your stroke.

How Burial Expense Companies Underwrite Strokes

When it comes to hell, there are three things to consider. Keep in mind; there is no funeral insurance company that will not question you ask about the stroke. That being said, below are three things that can affect pricing and policy regulations.

- Date of your last stroke.

- Medications that were prescribed because of your last stroke.

- Any physical or mental impairment resulting from a stroke.

In addition to the data points mentioned above, all of your other health conditions apply.

However, you don't have to worry.

You don't feel the need to figure out which option is best for stroke and other health problems.

That's why we are! We will collect all your information and decide which companies are best for you according to your health information.

The Importance of the Date Your Last Stroke was Diagnosed.

Some insurance companies will question you about when your last stroke was diagnosed, as a stroke usually happens again, and it is not known how serious it will be.

Most final cost insurance for full-blown stroke applications will be deferred for 12 months after the stroke is diagnosed. In fact, insurers are more likely to adopt policies with the highest premium rates.

In some cases, the minimum waiting period is two years. Your beneficiaries will only be entitled to the full death benefit if you pass away 24 months after approval.

We have insurers that offer immediate coverage from day one.

The companies will offer a better policy to cover final expenses or funeral insurance, but with a waiting period of at least two years. This applies to any type of stroke diagnosis in the last 24 months after application.

Health Questions

As you might know, every funeral insurance plan that has underwriting always come with health questions. Additionally, questions will be asked about the stroke in any of the formats below.

- Did you experienced, diagnosed, or treated for stroke in the past 12 months?

- Did you experienced, diagnosed, or treated for stroke in the past 24 months?

Keep in mind that insurance companies are much more likely to go as far as two years on strokes. It is only a few of them that seem to go only a year ago, but they are certainly in the minority.

Medications

Besides asking health problems, all final expense life insurance companies will monitor certain medications. In this case, they will follow a specific prescription that is usually used after someone has suffered a stroke.

Here are the most common stroke medications insurers look for

- Aggrenox

- Activase

- Coumadin

- Clopidogrel

- Nimotop

- Nimodipine

- Ticlid

- Plavix

- Warfarin

For stroke medications, the funeral insurance company will usually consider these three factors.

- The medications

- When was the first prescription issued?

- Is there a consistent filling since the first prescription?

Ultimately, keep all this information in mind when deciding if any medication will be a problem. If you have received any of these drugs for the first time in the last two years, many insurance agents will put you in the high-risk category (you will get a higher rate). At the same time, we have companies that perfectly accept these medications. Likewise, if you have been receiving any of these prescriptions for over two years, almost all insurance companies will stop holding them against you.

Finally, your Superior mutual agent will be able to tell you quickly and accurately if any of your medications will affect certain carriers' underwriting.

Physical Impairments

Unfortunately, physical impairment can be one of the worst disadvantages of a stroke. It is not uncommon for stroke victims to lose control of a body part. Sometimes it is permanent, and other times it is temporary. However, these side effects can prevent you from getting the most affordable rate possible.

So, this is the Conclusion.

It does not matter the circumstance you can get coverage. However, physical impairments caused by a stroke usually leads to other problems that can prevent you from getting immediate protection and high-risk the most affordable rate.

Life Insurance for Stroke Victims

Is it possible to get insurance after a TIA (minor stroke)? If you apply 24 months after your last stroke, top-rated insurers will offer Level policy options with the lowest payment rates. Also, with instant active insurance coverage that can come with some extra features.

Given the highly unpredictable nature of stroke, it would best that you or a loved one get an insurance on time.

Contact our final expense insurance experts, who have access to many top-rated insurance companies. We will professionally assist you in finding the best complete insurance policy for any stroke related condition for you or your loved ones.

What you expect If you have TIA or CVA

Funeral Insurance and Mini-Stroke

Will there be a waiting period for funeral insurance? Minor stroke or TIA as long as no permanent brain damage is done (which is not likely with a TIA), insurers will easily provide final expense insurance level policy.

This policy offers the best rates and immediate active insurance coverage that can have extra features.

Full-blown Stroke and Burial Insurance

Is there life insurance for you after having a stroke? As you may know, a full-blown stroke or CVA rather than a minor stroke is usually very serious and can lead to irreversible fatal injuries or death.

These are reasons insurers offer guaranteed issue policies to insure the final expense insurance for a CVA. This policy will have slightly higher pay rates and two years waiting period.

Activities of Daily Living (ADL's)

They are classified as bathing, dressing, eating, and going to the bathroom. If you need help with all these, it will be very difficult to get immediate coverage and the lowest rate. Generally, not all funeral insurance companies offer coverage to anyone who needs help with ADL.

Fortunately, we have access reputable Insurance company, who do not have a problem with applicants who need help in their daily lives and can provide level insurance policies with low payment rates and instant active coverage. Therefore, we hope that you will not have other health problems that would prevent you from qualifying.

Peradventure, you were not qualified for their coverage. We still have other top-rated companies that can offer another better option; however, the payment rate will be a little higher and with a waiting period of at least two years.

Home Health Care

It is highly common for stroke patients to need home health care for some time or permanently. However, like ADL, almost all funeral insurance companies ask specifically about home health care. Presently, if you are receiving home care, most insurers will decline.

Fortunately, there is a funeral insurance company that does not ask questions about home health care. They have no problem with it. If for any reason, you have other health problems that prevent you from getting qualified, your payment will be higher and will have to go through a waiting period.

Nursing Home

Depending on how severe the condition of your stroke, some patients need to be admitted to a nursing home when they are being rehabilitated. Unfortunately, you would not find a final expense company that does not specifically ask about a nursing home. No insurer will extend coverage to anyone who is presently in a nursing home.

So, if you are in a nursing home (regardless of the reason), your only option is to obtain a guaranteed issue life insurance policy. The premium is very small since they do not raise health questions, and it includes a two-year waiting period. Thanks to God, it is available because of your circumstance as it guarantees coverage.

Expectations for Stroke victims.

As you probably already know, the impact of a stroke on the cost of funeral insurance can be significant. In addition, a waiting period may be necessary, depending on when you last had a stroke. Here is a complete overview of what to expect based on the last time you had a stroke.

Your Stroke Has Occurred in the Last 12 Months.

Sadly, there will be an additional payment of about 15-30% and a waiting period of 2 years. Because your experience with stroke is recent, it is inevitable in every company.

Your Stroke Happened a Year Ago but in the Last Two Years.

In this case, there will be an improvement in your options. Mostly there are insurers who only asked about strokes in the last year. Because your stroke is over a year old, you can sincerely say no to this question. With these companies, you will be eligible for immediate insurance at the lowest prices.

Your Stroke Happened More than Two Years Ago.

Of course, many insurers will ask about strokes in the past two years. If yours is more than two years old, you can practically have a good option. Almost all companies do not care about the stroke because it is now beyond the scope of their guidelines. You will be eligible for Level rates. Your insurance will go into effect immediately, and you will have no waiting period.

How Much Life Insurance Should You Buy?

Before applying for life insurance, it would be best to decide the suitable policy for your family I case of any happening.

Some factors are important when figuring out the amount of life insurance that can effectively cover your family. Insufficient life insurance is one of the biggest mistakes you can make for your family members.

The first number you need to calculate is your bills and any debts you might be having currently. If something happens to you, all these costs and debts will go to your family.

Ensure that your life insurance policy is big enough to settle your mortgage, student debts, and other things that can burden your family.

The next number on your list to consider is your income per year. If something tragic happens to you, your family will not have your salary, meaning it would be difficult for them to pay basic expenses.

If you are one of the primary sources of income in your home, your life insurance plan must be big enough to replace your salary.

If you have suffered a stroke in the past years and you are seeking adequate and the best life insurance coverage, reach out to us and let's talk about your risk.

Ensure that all questions are answered in all sincerity and truthfully as possible to ensure you are not only getting the suitable level of coverage, but also the best rate available. The facts will be absolutely necessary for the agent providing the quote.

BURIAL INSURANCE AFTER A HEART ATTACK: A FULL BREAKDOWN

Did you know even if you've been declined from life insurance because of a recent heart attack, burial insurance is still available to you? Though burial insurance covers a smaller ranger of benefits than life insurance, it still envelops final expenses to ensure you or your beneficiaries are taken care of in their final moments. Furthermore, the persistent myth that burial insurance is outrageously expensive or borderline impossible after a heart attack is blatantly false. Affordable options are **always** available – never let an agent or insurance provider tell you otherwise. Though there may be a waiting period for full benefit, you do not have to declare bankruptcy to secure burial insurance.

In this article, we're going to look at what insurers look for in terms of coverage and how you can find the best option for both your financial and personal needs.

First and foremost, there are three types of coverage plans you could qualify for:

- Level benefit
- Graded
- Guaranteed issue

The policy you fall under depends on how many health issues you suffer from and most importantly, how much time has elapsed since your last heart attack. Carriers often work in the time frame of 12-24 months to determine your level of benefits. However, if your attack was more recent than a year, there are still options open to you. Let's go over each scenario:

If you are still being treated for a heart attack or had one within the last year, a waiting period of 2-3 years for full benefits is unavoidable. Nevertheless, you still may qualify for the **guaranteed issue.** The reason being is that these plans are the **only** ones available that require no medical underwriting (ie, mandatory health questioning). You would be charged 10% interest if the person insured passed away during the waiting period, but accidental health is covered from the moment you sign.

If you have multiple health conditions and are concerned no policy will want to take you on, don't worry! **Graded** policies are here for this reason. The carrier will pay a portion of the amount, increasing their disbursement each year, until the 4th year of coverage, when they will cover the full amount.

Note: Do NOT wait 2 years before getting a policy. In the event of another heart attack or unseen circumstance, you'll want to get covered as quickly as possible.

Let's say you're between 12 and 24 months. There are carriers that have these policies available, provided you do not have other health issues that would prevent qualification.

If your heart attack occurred over 24 months ago, you'll be treated as if you never had one at all: full benefit at the lowest price with no waiting period. This is the **level benefit** policy, very similar to level benefit life insurance plans. These plans are not permanent and are affordable with reliable costs.

Note: No matter the time frame, you will **never** be asked for a physical exam or EKG results.

It is important to understand that unless you have a guaranteed issue, insurance plans will require medical underwriting: a set of medical questions to uncover if you have any other health issue or risk in order to determine your coverage.

Let's Go More into More Depth of What Can be Expected in this Process:

Questions will vary depending on what specific provider you go to, but there are various ones that you can almost certainly expect to see, for example, if you suffer from any other severe medical conditions such as dialysis, cancer, congestive heart failure, Alzheimer's, as well as many other illnesses. They will inquire if you have a history of diabetes or high blood pressure, if you live in an assisted living facility, or if you can function on your own. Questions you may also want to consider are how many heart attacks you've had and if you've had any chest pains since your last attack.

One of the most prominent questions regards medications. Insurers will go over your prescription history. If you are on any sort of blood thinner, it will prompt a carrier to assume you have had a heart attack within their specified time frame. Subsequent questions can be quite detailed, including how often your medication is filled and if there have been any gaps in refills. Some companies will work with you regardless of your medications, including blood thinners, but will require extra analysis.

We've discussed different plans and what they require, but what about actually choosing a provider? With so many different insurance companies out there, it can be very difficult to know you're getting the best deal that serves you. You also hear about insurance scams and unreliable companies that either have horrific customer service, so your problems never get solved, or just take your money and run. There are a few things you can do about this.

One way to solve this dilemma is to find an agent, ideally one who specializes in burial insurance. This is an important distinction to make since many agents who do not know the field well will not be able to find a plan for you if your qualifications are abnormal or will try to saddle you with a guaranteed plan when you qualify for something better. Another reason a burial insurance agent is especially helpful is if your heart attack occurred between 12-24 months ago.

Most companies look at 2-3 years of your history, but there are specific ones that only go back a year. Your agent can help you find those few and far between companies, so you'll have a better plan while waiting out the extra year to qualify for full benefits and coverage. An agent can also help ensure you stay within budget and don't get caught up in extra, unexpected fees. Keep in mind that to find you the best plan, agents will most likely have a set of questions you'll need to answer, including but not limited to: the last time you had an attack, how many attacks you've had, if you've ever had a prescription for nitro pills, if you had to have surgery for your attack (and if so, when), as well as what specifically you were prescribed for your heart attack. Because there are scam artists out there, it is advisable to do heavy research before giving out any sort of personal information, medical or otherwise. Levison and Associates has a good reputation as an agency, as does Superior Mutual.

If finding an agent doesn't interest you, there are many companies that are well known specifically for their burial and funeral insurance policies you can look into on your own. Gerber Life Insurance, for instance, boasts great guaranteed plans – you'll get accepted no matter your health restrictions. Mutual of Omaha rates well in level benefit and graded policies – some of their plans even include added benefits at no additional cost. American Life Memorial and Lincoln Heritage also rate well in burial insurance policies.

Whatever you decide to do, make sure you do your research to ensure whomever you pick is best for YOU. The more knowledge you have, the better choice you'll make, and the quicker you'll know if someone isn't trustworthy. No matter your situation or when you had a heart attack, there is an option out there that will work for you. It's never fun, but necessary, and there are resources to help you with every step.

THE TRUTH ABOUT CARDIOMYOPATHY AND LIFE INSURANCE

Brutally Honest Guide to Burial Insurance with Cardiomyopathy

Are you seeking to get life insurance but wonder if your cardiomyopathy will cause you to be too high of a risk? If this sounds like you, you can drastically increase your odds of securing a good plan by applying with the best life insurance company from the start of your search. Though finding an affordable high-risk life insurance policy may seem complicated, you do not have to worry. We can guide you through this process.

In the following article, these are the key points you will learn about:

- Is It Possible to Secure Life Insurance with Cardiomyopathy?
- Cardiomyopathy, what is it?
- What Causes Cardiomyopathy?
- Are There Different Types of Cardiomyopathy and What Are They?
- Medications Commonly Used to Treat Cardiomyopathy
- How to Get Life Insurance with Cardiomyopathy
- What Should be Expected When Getting Life Insurance with Cardiomyopathy?
- Where to Proceed to Secure the Best Rates for Life Insurance with Cardiomyopathy

What are the Primary Points to Take Away From this Article?

Life insurance providers consider cardiomyopathy to be a high-risk condition. This means that a "flat extra" charge will likely be added to your premiums if you are approved for coverage. The cost can be an average of 25% or higher.

When life insurance companies evaluate high-risk conditions, such as heart disease, there is no blanket policy that they can offer. That being said, our knowledgeable agents know how to navigate the sea of life insurance companies to find one that serves best for your situation.

Our years of experience mean that we will find the life insurance company that is most suitable for your health condition.

Using the incorrect life insurance company has caused many people to have a hard time getting covered with an affordable premium.

Because of our background, we know precisely which life insurance companies to go to when seeking a life insurance plan with consideration of cardiomyopathy for you.

Now, let us cover some of the most commonly asked questions when applying for life insurance with cardiomyopathy.

Is It Possible to Secure Life Insurance with Cardiomyopathy?

To answer one of the most asked questions when applying for any life insurance plan: absolutely. You will want to take care of and understand a few things before you start, but it is possible. One of the first and most essential items a life insurance company will ask for is your most recent ECG results. This should be presented in an orderly fashion. Family history, whether you smoke, your weight, and blood pressure are all determinants that life insurance companies will consider in your application process. But do not worry. It is possible to get life insurance coverage with cardiomyopathy.

Cardiomyopathy, what is it?

Cardiomyopathy is a condition that causes your heart to have a more challenging time pumping blood to the remainder of your body because it has become enlarged or thicker. This means that your heart has a more difficult time keeping a regular electric rhythm.

Cardiomyopathy can impair the heart and lead to arrhythmias, congestive heart failure, heart valve problems, or other conditions over time.

What Causes Cardiomyopathy?

In children, the cause of the cardiomyopathy is typically unknown. Sometimes this is the case with adults as well. Occasionally, the condition is inherited. Otherwise, it is the result of other health conditions. Though not an exhaustive list, here are several of the ailments that can lead to cardiomyopathy:

- Long-term alcohol abuse
- Long-term drug abuse, specifically stimulants
- Long-term high blood pressure
- Being obese
- Other heart conditions

Are There Different Types of Cardiomyopathy and What Are They?

The most common varieties of cardiomyopathy include:

- Arrhythmogenic right ventricular dysplasia (ARVD)
- Dilated cardiomyopathy (DCM)
- Hypertrophic cardiomyopathy (HCM)
- Restrictive cardiomyopathy (RCM)
- Transthyretin amyloid cardiomyopathy (ATTR-CM)
- Unclassified cardiomyopathy (this includes "broken-heart syndrome")

Medications Commonly Used to Treat Cardiomyopathy

The most prescribed medications are:

- Angiotensin-converting enzyme (ACE) inhibitors
- Angiotensin II receptor blockers
- Beta-blockers
- Blood-thinners
- Digoxin (or Digitalis)
- Diuretics

Considering that cardiomyopathy is sometimes fatal, it is understandable that an underwriter would want to discover as much as they can about your heart disease. When determining your life insurance classification, which then, in turn, determines if you do get your preferred rates, all of these separate details are considered.

How to Get Life Insurance with Cardiomyopathy

All cases are unique when it comes to heart disease. It is because of this that we will need to know the answers to these questions to ensure that you receive the most desirable rates possible:

- When did you receive your first diagnosis?
- Does your medical history include fainting or dizziness, palpitations, shortness of breath, or angina?
- What did your last ECG report contain?
- What medications, if any, are you currently taking?
- What surgeries have you had, if any: heart surgery, pacemaker, or defibrillator procedures?
- How often have you smoked, if at all, in the last three years?
- Do you have any other additional health conditions?

We may get the most accurate rates, it will help if you are as detailed as possible about your health history. Since we can work with over

60 life insurance companies, we can most certainly find the best possible rates for you. None of these companies receive preferential treatment. Whichever company presents the best option for your situation is the one that we will send your way. The only way we can confirm that it is the best policy for you is to know that we have received the most unbiased, detailed information from you. Underwriters will be able to confirm your information after combing through your medical records.

What Should be Expected When Getting Life Insurance with Cardiomyopathy?

It is not impossible to get a "standard" health classification with a cardiomyopathy diagnosis in your medical history, but it is difficult. To be qualified for this, you must have completely recovered from your cardiomyopathy or have been stable for at least six months, have a normal ECG, have no other severe health conditions, and have no lifestyle factors that could lead to another occurrence of cardiomyopathy.

If you meet the above requirements, you are more likely to receive a "Table 2" policy offer. We can help explain this if you need us to, call us. If you do not satisfy those qualifications, your coverage will depend on your situation. Unfortunately, as the severity of your condition increases, so do your rates.

But life insurance is not your only option. Another route to take is a guaranteed life insurance plan if the available coverage is unaffordable for you. No health information will be required to approve one of these plans, but you will get less coverage, and it will not go into effect until after 24 months. If the unfortunate happens during those two years, your premiums plus 10% will be returned. With companies like Gerber Life Insurance and AIG can insure you for up to $35,000, so as an alternative to a pricier life insurance plan, these are ones to consider.

Where to Go to Secure the Best Rates for Life Insurance with Cardiomyopathy

With the expertise we offer, you will be comforted knowing that you will receive the tailored experience that your condition deserves. It would help if you did not have to find a policy on your own.

What are the Next Steps to Take?

We can help you purchase your life insurance. There are several different ways to contact us, so that we may start that process:

- Online
- Call us
- Fill out a physical application and send it in through the mail

Legend Guide to Buying Burial Insurance with Angina

Angina is challenging to deal with on its own, but what happens when you need to purchase final expense insurance with a history of chest pains? How does that diagnosis affect your plan? Is there a way to buy burial insurance without having to figure the complicated process on your own?

Many companies out there will entertain the idea and even work with you to find a plan, to leave you with declined coverage or overly inflated prices. We at Superior Mutual can do better than that. With years of experience and loads of insurance companies to compare, we can find the perfect, most cost-effective plan for you and your health situation. We are here to help ease the burden of finding final expense insurance on your own.

To help you understand the steps we, or any insurance company, will take, we have put together an easy-to-understand guide on what to expect during this process. If you still have questions after reading our thorough guide, do not hesitate to call us at 1-888-810-9725. We will be happy to assist you in learning the ins and outs of purchasing a final expense insurance policy.

Burial Coverage and Angina

Have you had treated for chest pains in the past two years? Unfortunately, a diagnosis of angina will result in higher burial insurance premiums in almost all circumstances. Rarely will this not be the result, and depending on the details of your condition, will determine your options.

All in all, a slightly elevated premium and a twenty-four-month waiting period is likely the most unfavorable situation to come against in the quest to find burial insurance with angina. Most importantly, you will still be able to get affordable final expenses insurance. There are some infrequent occasions where securing coverage with immediate benefits at roughly the same rate as a healthy person is possible, but this is not typical.

But here is the good news: you will only have to answer a few questions about your health. When applying for burial insurance, there will be no need to take a physical or medical examination or even provide any medical records.

Our job is risk assessment. At Superior Mutual, we review the answers to our questions that you provide to find the most dependable, most affordable insurance company for you.

Angina and Underwriting

When considering insurance companies to purchase final expense insurance, you should note that all will include questions about chest pains in their underwriting. This also means that they will be reviewing any medications involved in the treatment of angina.

Each company will have very similar questions about chest pains. All of them will primarily involve two components:

- the chest pains themselves.

- the medications used to treat the chest pains.

These details will help the insurance company assess which coverage option is right for you.

What does it mean to treat angina?

For funeral insurance companies, the treatment of angina does not mean the taking of the prescribed medications. It only means the filling of certain prescribed medications.

The assumption is that if you have gone to the pharmacist to have a prescription filled, you are taking that medication. The insurance companies will ask when you filled your prescription so that an accurate history of your condition can be considered on the previously mentioned health questionnaire.

A typical example of this is when a doctor hands out a prescription for nitroglycerin as a rescue drug. Filling this drug will put you in the same category as someone who recently experienced chest pains and treated it. As there is no practical way to follow whether or not you consumed the prescription, the matter is black and white for the insurance company. You were essentially treated for angina, regardless of if you were treated for a chest pain event. You needed the medication if you filled the prescription, in their opinion.

What Are Some Prescriptions that Burial Insurance Companies Will Monitor During this Process?

Certain medications are prescribed to treat angina, as listed below:

• Amyl Nitrate*

• Corgard

• Dilatrate SR*

• Aspirin

• Heparin

• Imdur*

• Ismo

• IsoDitrate

- Isochron

- Isordil*

- Isosorbide Dinitrate/Mononitrate*

- Lovenox

- Minitran*

- Monoket

- Nitrek

- Nitro-bid*

- Nitro-dur*

- Nitroglycerine*

- Nitroquick*

- Nitrostat*

- Nitrol*

- Nitromist*

- Ranexa*

- Ranolazine

- Vascor*

If the only prescriptions you take are the medications with an asterisk (*) beside them in the above list and you have not recently (the last two-years) experienced any angina, then you will be qualified for a regular plan. This means no higher than typical rates or long wait times.

What are Some Questions Regarding Chest Pains That Insurance Companies Ask During the Underwriting Process?

Typically, insurance companies will ask questions concerning a specific period. The purpose is to get a better understanding of the potential severity of the condition. Most of the time, one of the following formats will be applied to ask these questions:

1. Have you been treated for chest pains (angina) within the last 24 months?

2. Have you been treated for chest pains (angina) within the last 12 months?

Once those questions have been answered, new options will appear based on your answers. In answering the next set of questions, it is essential to consider that angina treatment typically causes most people problems. Below is some information concerning each of the possible options:

You Have Had or Been Treated for Chest Pains in the Last 12 Months?

A diagnosis of angina within a year of applying for final expense insurance will guarantee a plan with a two-year waiting period and a higher cost than a healthy person, as insurance companies will consider you a higher risk. Considering the severity of having chest pains, the best insurance plan will be the cheaper option of a guaranteed issue plan from Sons of Norway. This plan will also come with a twenty-four-month waiting period.

You Have Had or Been Treated for Chest Pains Within the Last 24 Months but Not Within the Last 12 Months?

As the time removed from the chest pain event lengthens, your options will improve. Since many companies only care about angina within the last year, you will be considered similar to a person in perfect health and fully covered from day one if it has been longer than a year since the last time you experienced angina.

Your Chest Pains & Treatment Were Over 2 Years Ago

Again, as this period is over two years since you experienced chest pains, virtually all burial insurance companies will cover you with no wait time and at the same affordable rate as a person in good health. Few companies will even ask about angina after two years.

Still Taking Angina Medications Even Though Your Chest Pains Were Years Ago?

Earlier in this article, we discussed how final expense insurance companies consider prescriptions. This same idea applies here. It will be as if the actual chest pain event happened at the last time you had the pharmacist fill the drug, as there is no way to track when you take the medication.

What is the Best Way to Find the Most Suitable Burial Insurance with Angina?

With any medical condition, securing burial insurance is challenging without the proper guidance of an insurance professional. As you can tell, this is no different for angina. Working with Superior Mutual will allow you to understand your situation's options more effectively with access to many burial insurance companies. Our experience working with individuals like you enables us to narrow the field of plan options to compare the best ones for you.

There is no question that you could find a great final expense insurance plan on your own, or even work with a different brokerage company to find an excellent plan for you. If you choose to take this path, do not forget to confirm that the company you choose to work with represents many insurance companies and has extensive experience working with individuals with a history of chest pains.

We hope that you permit us to work for you. If you choose to, we would love to quickly help you find the best final insurance policy for you. To start looking for your best final expense insurance plan, fill out the quote form below, and we will call you shortly. Or go ahead and call us at 1-888-810-9725, and we will start working for you immediately.

SUREFIRE WAY TO GET BURIAL INSURANCE AFTER TIA ATTACK

At the moment, you may think that it will be very difficult to get affordable funeral insurance after a TIA attack.

And you would be right to think like that.

Securing the lowest rate for funeral insurance is completely possible, even if you have a TIA attack.

It turns out that there are end-of-life expense companies that are very okay with accepting applicants who had experienced a mini-stroke. We have helped a lot of applicants in the past to obtain funeral plans after a TIA attack. Today, we will reveal how we helped them.

In this article, we will show how funeral insurers will respond to a mini stroke, what their options will be, and how to get the best plan possible.

Is Life Insurance Possible If I Had Experienced a Stroke?

Why do End-of-life expense companies or Burial insurers consider applicants with Mini-Stroke?

Can I get life insurance after a stroke? This is because a mini-stroke or transient ischemic attack (TIA) is generally not fatal and generally does not cause permanent damage to the brain of the brain or any disability after suffering a mini-stroke.

Give attention to the symptoms; if you have uncontrolled high blood pressure, you may have a stroke.

According to studies, people who have suffered a small stroke are more likely to live longer with a healthier lifestyle than would be expected, despite being called a Stroke.

Therefore, the conclusion is that if you apply for end-of-life insurance after a mini-stroke and you are living a healthy life and do not suffer any serious damage after a mini-stroke.

The best policy is the Level type, with low payment rates, instant insurance coverage without a waiting period, and additional innovative features, with no additional costs available from top-rated life insurers.

So, if you are a candidate with a mini stroke, do not sign up with any insurance company. You will need top-rated insurers with the best extra benefits. We do our best in this regard, ensure you contact one of our end-of-life specialists.

Expectations When Purchasing Burial Insurance After Having a TIA Attack

Each end-of-life insurance plan will ask specifically about strokes. However, mini strokes are very different from the full blow strokes. As a result, we are excited to report that there are some funeral insurers that will not question you about transient ischemic attacks.

Since there are life insurers who do not ask about mini strokes, you may be fully eligible for a simplified death funeral insurance plan. This means that you will pay the lowest total cost offered by the life insurance company, and your coverage will take effect on the day one of your policy. There won't be any waiting period.

And This is Good News for You

You will not need to provide a blood or urine sample at any time during the application process. There is no medical examination. All that is required of you is to answer some health questions. Some insurers are concerned about a mini-stroke and, of course, charge more and impose a waiting period. Luckily for you, you are dealing with an independent agency that is highly experienced and has access to many funeral insurers. We will connect you with one of our insurance companies that would not care about mini stroke.

Underwriting for Transient Ischemic Attack

There is no end-of-life insurance company that does not ask about full-blown strokes. At the same time, many of them will ask about mini strokes. Luckily, there are some companies that don't ask about it, and it doesn't matter if you've had one.

With a transient ischemic attack, a small blood clot in the brain briefly interferes with blood flow. The net result of this temporary barrier is not permanent damage. This is completely different from a full-blown stroke, where the blockage is not temporal, and the damage is usually permanent.

Finally, the lack of permanent damage is why funeral insurers do not view the TIA as a high-risk incident. However, some insurance companies will do this.

The conclusion here is.

Your options will depend on whether you will be eligible for a funeral insurance plan with one of the insurers that are not concerned with the transient ischemic attack. If you have other health issues that will make you ineligible, your options are very bleak. If this happens, it is still possible for you to obtain an affordable policy; however, there will be some concessions.

The health questions about mini stroke will be similar to the ones listed below:

- Have you undergone any treatment for TIA attack in the past two years?

- Have you undergone any treatment for TIA attack during the last 12 months?

It is not uncommon for the end-of-life expense company to inquiry about mini-strokes in the last two years. Anyway, some life insurance companies will only check back as far as one year for mini-strokes and full-blown strokes.

The Effect the Date of Your Last Stroke Has on Your Burial Insurance Options

From here, there will be frequent mention of insurance companies that are not okay with mini-stroke applicants.

Insurers take into account the date of the applicant's last minor stroke and essentially classify the candidates according to the dates of the candidate's stroke and their rules.

The Applicant's Mini-Stroke Has Occurred in the Last 12 Months

For most insurers, applicants who fall into this category are at great risk. Most insurers offer insurance policies for funeral insurance with the highest payment rates and a minimum waiting period of 2 years.

The Applicant Suffered a Mini-Stroke in the Last 12 Months of 24 Months Ago

If you are in this category will get better offers from insurers. The final cost insurance offers in this category will have better payment rates but will have a waiting period of at least two years to fully release death benefits.

The Applicant Suffered a Mini-Stroke Over 24 Months Ago

Applicants in this category generally receive the best insurance for final costs, which is a Simplified or level policy with an affordable payment rate, no waiting period, and instant active coverage.

Now, where do you fall? Is it the first or second category? Contact our closing funeral insurance experts to get the lowest price and possibly without a waiting period from a top-rated insurers' and approval on the same day.

Medications That You Need to Watch Out with Companies That Are Concerned with Mini Strokes

Besides the health questions, the history of the prescription is always being checked. Essentially, the insurer will be checking for a known drug that treats the condition. In a situation like this, they will be aware of some common medications that are usually prescribed after a mini stroke. Almost all of them have blood thinners of some type.

If you take any of these drugs due to a Transient ischemic Attack, you would expect some funeral insurance companies to treat you as a mini-stroke patient. Even if you are saying NO to the health question about TIA, these medications will surely go against your answer.

Each insurance company is a different type of guide for drugs. You only need to know that these are usually on the insurer's lookout. After all, these medications are much more than these; however, these are the well-known ones.

What you need to know is that your agent will be completely aware of this. We just love sharing information with people, and that's why we have to go over them.

- Aggrenox

- Nimodipine

- Activas

- Mimotope

- Clopidogrel

- Tic lid

- Plavix

Discover the Lowest Cost Burial Insurance with a Defibrillator

Based on what you will see on most websites on life insurance, it is very difficult to get affordable funeral insurance with a defibrillator.

However, it is Merely a Myth.

Yes, it is. It really is a myth. Large premiums do not automatically mean funeral insurance if you have a defibrillator.

You do not automatically have to pay high funeral insurance premiums if you have a defibrillator.

The truth is that you can sign up for a final life insurance plan that will not go beyond your budget. All through the years, we have helped many people with defibrillators do that. Now, we will reveal you how we helped them and also open your eyes to these secrets.

In this article, we will talk about the typical insurance company underwriting process for applicants with defibrillators. Your available option and how to get the best defibrillator funeral insurance.

Implantable Cardioverter Defibrillator (ICD) and Final Expense Insurance Companies

Let's begin with the bad news.

Either you believe it or not, having an ICD insurer is not something many insurance companies see as a problem.

Even though it is true that having a CID is not a problem for funeral insurers, there are certain circumstances that may affect your chances of being offered a basic price for immediate coverage.

In addition to other serious illnesses that insurers may have a problem with, there are often ICD cases that can impact the quality and price of the coverage plans offered.

Many insurers would have a problem with you if you recently installed the ICD or replaced the battery – you will see more on this in the ICD underwriting process.

Other Good News

Many final expense insurers will not ask if you have an Implantable Cardioverter Defibrillator or ICD, or, as people call it, a heart defibrillator implant - they don't even talk about it in their underwriting questions. This means that they are not looking for it, and it's perfectly okay with these insurers.

In addition, you do not need to undergo a medical or physical examination to obtain a funeral or final expense insurance.

We have helped many clients get a basic funeral insurance plan with immediate coverage on the first day - insurers often call this plan simplified, preferred, or level.

So, you might be asking, does that automatically mean I am qualified for a simplified or level plan?"

Not yet, in order to get the lowest cost with immediate protection, you must first go through an underwriting process.

Final Expense Insurance Company Underwriting process for ICD.

The underwriting process usually occurs when funeral insurance companies or closing costs want to find out if there are other illnesses, health problems, alcohol, or tobacco consumption, etc. They will also ask you questions about your lifestyle and analyze the history of medication prescriptions.

Basically, insurers will assess every aspect of your health to classify your risk level and determine what type of insurance coverage you can get.

- How far do life insurers examine medical records?

- During the underwriting process, insurers will question about the following:

- Questions about your current and previous diseases (if any) and your lifestyle.

- Evaluation of the history of prescription drugs.

Health Questions

While asking questions in the underwriting process, all insurers will ask about all types of diseases that typically have a low chance of survival based on statistics. Tobacco use and alcohol consumption are also essential, as they can exacerbate any disease or shorten a person's life expectancy.

NOTE: the text of the underwriting question varies from one insurer to another.

Answering health questions may be simple, but don't try to answer them yourself! To answer these questions, consulting an insurance specialist experienced in final costs can make the difference between paying cheaply or highly.

In any case, when you get the best insurance plan for the funeral or closing cost, you need to contact an expert in insurance to guide you specifically from the beginning.

An independent agent who is experienced in the underwriting process with an insurance company will have a good understanding will know immediately which insurance company will best take care of your health.

We will only need a bit of your time to get your details.

Specific Questions about ICD

Now, we definitely realize that you have an implantable cardioverter-defibrillator (ICD). There will be more questions about the ICD.

- When did you have your ICD installation?

- Have you ever replaced your ICD battery? If yes, when?

- Why did you need an ICD?

- What other health condition have you had in the past two years?

- What are the medications you are taking for other diseases?

Your answers to the questions above will determine what type of coverage you will be qualified for.

Burial Insurance Companies Offer for ICD.

If you have recently had heart or circulatory surgery, it will affect how much you pay and whether or you are getting a waiting period for your policy or not. Keep in mind that there are dozens and dozens of end-of-life companies that may be less interested in whether or not you have a defibrillator. The only problem you had to worry about is the installation time. Below you will see the impact of your CDI installation date if any.

Your Defibrillator Was Installed Last Year.

In this case, your payment for the monthly premium will be higher and have a two-year waiting period for the policy. Sadly, it is impossible to prevent this. Thankfully, you can still obtain a policy, and it won't cost you beyond the ordinary. Your price will usually be about 15 to 30% higher than the monthly premium of a healthy person.

The Installation of Your Defibrillator Happened Over Two Years Ago.

At a point like this, you are at an advantage. You can easily get a simplified death benefit from many funeral insurance companies. Your rates will be the lowest possible and your protection instantly from the first day of the policy because your got ICD installed over two years ago.

Battery changes?

Battery replacement involves simple and relatively small outpatient surgery. To be sincere, some insurers will see this procedure as cardiac or circulatory surgery. Along with them, you will have to pay a higher premium and stay in a waiting period if it is recent.

Simultaneously, we certainly have funeral insurance companies that do not consider replacing an ICD battery as qualified for cardiac or circulatory surgery. If you have recently changed your battery, we will send you to one of these companies to get an instant benefit and the affordable price they offer. It's nice to have options, isn't it?

How You Can Get the Best Burial Insurance if You Are an Applicant with ICD

When it comes to DCI coverage, you should pay attention to the following qualities:

- The insurer has the most affordable monthly premium.

- An insurer that offers a simplified and looks back as far as 12-month on ICD installation.

- The insurer can provide a simplified plan, regardless of whether you have an ongoing ICD battery change.

- The policy has the greatest benefit rewards with instant coverage.

- The insurer is stable financially and has proven experience.

We can provide you with these coverage qualities for any applicants with ICD. We have helped many people with ICDs - even those who have installed their own for more than 12 months but under 24 months or whose ICD battery has recently been replaced.

Life Insurance for Mitral Valve Prolapse: The Easy Way to be Approved

Have you ever been diagnosed with mitral valve prolapse? Even if mitral valve prolapse is considered high-risk life insurance, we will help you get a life insurance at an affordable rate.

Mitral valve prolapse is a very common medical condition, and under appropriate conditions, it is eligible for the best life insurance health classification: plus option. Our role is to help you apply to a life insurance company with the best mitral valve prolapse. At Superior Mutual, we have helped many clients find the best life insurance rates through mitral valve prolapse. We know the underwriter's concerns and understand which company offers the best deals.

- Mitral Valve Prolapse (MVP) and life insurance: the insurer's view.

- Mitral Valve Prolapse (MVP) Life insurance rating examples.

- Guaranteed Issue Life with Mitral valve prolapse (MVP)

- Get the best MVP life insurance rates.

Life Insurance is Not Exciting. Let Us Look at the Basics! These Are Our Observations.

You might get life insurance for mitral valve prolapse, and life insurance companies will even provide you with preferential rates.

The thickness of the mitral valve, the degree of MR (mitral regurgitation), and the left atrium size are the three most important factors while applying.

Mitral Valve Prolapse and Life Insurance: An Insurer's Perspective

The three most important factors that life insurance insurers need to consider are:

1. The rate and presence of mitral regurgitation

2. Mitral valve viscosity

3. The size of left atrium

This data can be found on your EKGs.

You need to know these factors when looking for the cheapest life insurance for mitral valve prolapse or any heart disease. However, there's no problem if you don't know. Mos of our clients don't know the specifics. In this case, we will apply for the preferred life insurance rate from the carriers with the best offer (assuming no other health issues). The detailed information will be listed in the underwriting; if necessary, we can switch and apply to other life insurance companies at any time.

Examples of Life Insurance Ratings for Mitral Valve Prolapse

Let's take a look at three life insurance cases with mitral valve prolapse so that you can understand the expected types of life insurance rates.

Case 1:

The electrocardiogram (EKG) showed a normal appearance of the mitral valve prolapse, with no signs of mitral regurgitation and normal left atrium. There are no other potential health problems.

This situation is eligible for the best fare class available: "Preferred Plus."

Case 2:

The electrocardiogram (EKG) showed a slight thickening of mitral valve prolapse, a normal left atrium, and mild regurgitation. Because the valve is slightly thickened, the left atrium is normal, and there are no other potential health problems, we suggest a "Standard Plus" offer for this case.

Case 3:

Their electrocardiogram (EKG) showed excessive mitral valve, moderate mitral regurgitation, and left atrium dilation. Because of the enlargement of the left atrium, this will be "substandard" life insurance. The actual rating will depend on your age and left atrium enlargement. On the off chance that you have moderate to extreme mitral valve prolapse, you need to record a good follow-up ECG to show the stability record of the past few years (preferably more than five years).

Guaranteed Life insurance Issues for Mitral Valve Prolapse

Although life insurance with mitral valve prolapse is approved in most cases, you still encounter circumstances that make it a bit challenging for you to obtain traditional life insurance. Usually, this happens when you have a health condition other than mitral valve prolapse. If this happens, you do not necessarily have to give up all coverage for you and your family. Life insurance can always be considered. The coverage provided by rating companies such as Gerber Life and AIG requires no medical inquiry or medical examination to be approved. Make sure to compare all options with your agent, including guaranteed acceptance life insurance.

Get the Best Life Insurance Price for Mitral Valve Prolapse.

Several life insurance companies offer better deals to people with mitral valve prolapse than other life insurance companies. The bottom line is that you should apply to one of these companies. Our connections with the leading life insurance companies in the market and our experience in reducing mitral valve underwriting give us a competitive advantage over other institutions. We always replace new policies with cheaper options simply because we are using the right life insurance company. If you are interested in offers based on your risks, all we have to do is enter your health status over the phone. Our agents never have any obligation or pressure. We'll only provide you with the information you need and respond to all your queries.

Burial Insurance for People with Atrial Fibrillation - Get the Facts Here

According to the CDC between 2.7 million and 6.7 million people in the United States suffer from a cardiac condition known as Atrial Fibrillation. It is the most common type of heart arrhythmia.

Atrial fibrillation is often referred to as A-Fib. A-Fib causes irregular heartbeats A-Fib is associated with several risk factors. It can even develop simply because you are aging. For most people with atrial fibrillation their doctors prescribe a medication that helps to control their heart rhythms.

Atrial fibrillation causes real trouble for people who are trying to buy burial insurance. The insurance companies see the diagnosis of A-Fib on your medical records and they either refuse to insure you or they offer you insurance at rates that you cannot afford.

It is very frustrating to know that you need burial insurance so that your family is not burdened when you pass and be unable to find coverage that you can afford.

There is an answer to this problem. A diagnosis of A-Fib does not mean that you are never going to be able to find burial insurance.

Why do Insurance Companies Charge More for or Refuse Insurance to People with A-Fib?

A-Fib is not the real problem as far as the insurance company is concerned. The insurance company knows that A-Fib can be an underlying cause to other conditions like strokes and heart attacks.

They also know that people who have been diagnosed with A-Fib often have other serious medical conditions.

Insurance companies do not want to take a risk of losing money. They want to insure people who are going to pay their premiums and not cost the insurance company. They are happiest with really healthy people who will pay premiums for many years before the insurance company has to pay the coverage amount named in the burial insurance policy.

People with serious heart conditions, like A-Fib, or heart failure are people who could die before the insurance company makes enough money off their premiums to make the final payment not cost them money.

Looking for the Right Coverage

You know by now that the best way to shop for things like insurance coverage is to compare several offers. You weigh the pros and cons of each policy, and then you can decide which policy is best for you.

Looking for insurance is a hassle. There is just no other way to put it. You either call the insurance company, or you visit their website. Then you answer a multitude of questions. Finally, you give the company your phone number and email address, and they promise to get back with you when they have your quote ready.

You wait hours, or days, to hear back from each of the companies you have spoken to.

The insurance companies either get in touch with you and tell you that they cannot offer you any coverage, or they offer you coverage that is less than you want at a price that is more than you are willing to pay.

Prepare to Look for Insurance.

Most people do not know that insurance companies often ask trick questions in an effort to get people to reveal something about their medical history. They may ask you if you have any cardiac issues, but they may slip the question about cardiac issues in via other questions.

Some of the medical questions used by insurance companies to uncover A-Fib are:

- Have you ever had rapid heartbeats?

- Have you ever had a stroke?

- Have you ever had a heart attack?

These questions by themselves cannot cause the insurance company to believe you have atrial fibrillation, but questions like these, and the list of medications you take, can cause them to believe it.

You have to be prepared for the medical questions, and the tricky medical questions when you are searching for insurance. You have to tell the truth about your health conditions, or the insurance policy will not be honored when you pass. You cannot hide an illness like A-Fib, but you can answer the questions carefully so the agency will offer you better plans.

Final Expense Insurance Specialist

We offer final expense insurance specialists to help you navigate the medical questions associated with burial insurance. These specialists need to know the absolute truth about your medical condition so they can help you answer the underwriter questions truthfully without sending up insurance red flags.

Our specialist sees the insure underwriter questions daily. They know what kind of answers the company is looking for, and they know what kind of answers a person with A-Fib will have to give. They have learned through experience how to answer the question without making the condition seem worse than it is.

The final expense insurance specialists will know what medications are going to cause the insurance agency to believe your condition is worse than it is.

Your Medicine Reveals a Lot about Your Health

The medication that you take tells an insurance company or medical professional a lot about your current health issues and possible future health issues.

If you take some medications the insurance company will automatically consider you to be an -Fib patient. These medicines include:

- Amiodarone (Cordarone or Pacerone)
- Digitek
- Digoxin
- Dofetilide
- Flecainide (Tambocor)
- Lanoxicaps
- Lanoxin
- Propafenone (Rythmol)
- Quinidine (Various)
- Sotalol (Betapace)
- Warfarin

Insurance companies may tell you that you do not have to see a doctor or get a physical to get coverage. That is because they are going to take your answers to what medicine you take, and what health issues you have, and they are then going to make up their own mind on whether or not they think you suffer from a serious condition like A-Fib.

Even if you take none of those medications, the fact that you take a high blood pressure medication can often cause insurance agents to be suspicious of your health answers.

Why We Can Help A-Fib Patients Find Burial Insurance

We only deal with top rated A+ insurance companies that can offer our clients the final expense insurance they are searching for. We do not waste our clients time, or our time, dealing with insurance companies that offer people with medical conditions like A-Fib poor coverage at extravagant cost.

Our team of final insurance specialist work hard to create a list of insurance companies that offer fair priced insurance. They know which companies offer the best coverage and they have a vast amount of experience so they can walk you through the application process quickly.

The main reason why we are able to help you get great insurance at a fair price is our experience. Our company founder has more than 35 years' experience in dealing with burial insurance providers. Our specialist only works with people who are trying to get burial insurance and the majority of our clients have a medical condition like A-Fib that can stop them from getting good insurance coverage.

A Vast Network

In order for us to be able to help people with medical conditions like Atrial fibrillation find burial insurance that is good, and fair priced we had to develop a vast network of insurance companies. Most companies that help you look for burial insurance will only have a few companies that will work with people who have health issues.

That means their clients have a limited number of options for their insurance coverage. The list of insurance companies we have that works with people who have medical conditions is vast. The multiple insurance companies mean that you will get multiple offers for coverage, and you will have options in your coverage.

One call

All you have to do is give us a call and let us go to work for you. You will answer medical questions one time, and then we will answer all of the different insurance companies.

We will ask you if you suffer from A-Fib. We will ask you what medication you take. We will find an insurance company that does not discriminate against your condition.

There is no reason for you to worry any longer about your burial insurance. We have an answer for you, and we actually want to help you.

A Final Thought

We know that hunting for burial insurance is frustrating. I am stressful and it is not something anyone enjoys doing. Let out specialist sit down with you and help you through this process. They can find you coverage you can afford, and they will do so cheerfully.

You do not need to be punished for having a health condition. Atrial fibrillation is hard enough for you to deal with without you feeling like you are being punished and are not going to be able to take care of your final expenses. You need someone who understands what you are going through and who is capable of helping you find real solutions.

We have a success rate of finding burial insurance policies that have no waiting periods for as many as 90% of our clients. Our clients get insurance coverage at the lowest possible cost, and all they have to do is invest a few minutes of time with one of our agents over the phone.

The Secret to Low Cost Burial Insurance with High Blood Pressure

You might be thinking that it will be difficult for you to qualify for a funeral insurance plan with high blood pressure. We are happy to tell you that high blood pressure will not stop you in any way when looking for funeral insurance.

It Keeps Getting Better

Even if you have uncontrolled high blood pressure, we can easily get qualified for instant benefits.

In this article, we are going to show you how insurance companies react to hypertension and how you can get the best insurance if you have high blood pressure.

And you don't want to miss this good news....

Because funeral insurance plans are simplified, you do not need a physical or medical examination. You just have to answer a few health questions.

If Your Blood Pressure is Under Control

What is considered as life insurance for high blood pressure? They type of blood pressure that is uncontrollable by medications will be a concern for life insurance. However, if it can be controlled by medication and monitored, then you should not worry; any insurance company will attend to you immediately! You can choose any final expense insurer, and they will be willing to offer you an insurance policy.

But you wouldn't need just any insurance, would you?

The truth is that if you haven't managed your hypertension in the past two years.

For some reason, high blood pressure has not been controlled in the past two years.

Don't worry, although there are some insurance companies that will charge you more for candidates with hypertension or high blood pressure.

There are some premium rate insurers that offer the lowest payment with instant insurance coverage.

What You Need to Know About Same Day Policy for High Blood Pressure

This means there would not be a waiting period.

Basically, dealing only with high blood pressure is not a problem for the world-class funeral or end-of-life insurer.

So, to make sure you get the best deal, you need to contact a specialist who is experienced in end-of-life insurance, who only has access to those best A + insurers.

No physical examination or review of medical history. Only a few questions, no problem!

But hold on, it is not always this simple for everyone ...

Another crucial thing to keep in mind is that uncontrolled hypertension can cause stroke and heart attack. It is always advisable to consult your doctor regularly.

- History of prescribed burial life insurance drugs

- Medications marked by insurance companies

Have you been denied life insurer prescription history? There are certain medications that insurers are looking for while assessing candidates with high blood pressure.

Some insurance companies will classify you as a high risk if you take any of the medications below.

- Amlodipine
- Atenolol
- Amyl Nitrate
- Betaxolol
- Bisoprolol fumarate
- Bumetanide
- Candesartan
- Carteolol
- Carvedilol
- Chlorthalidone
- Coreg
- Diltiazem
- Diovan
- Doxazosin Mesylate
- Esmolol
- Furosemide
- Indapamide
- Labetalol
- Lasix

- Hydrochlorothiazide
- Lisinopril
- Losartan
- Losartan
- Lopressor
- Metoprolol
- Monoket
- Nadolol
- Nebivolol
- Nicardipine
- Nifedipine
- Norvasc
- Spironolactone

There are many medications for high blood pressure that some insurance companies are concerned with. This may be due to side effects or long-term effects of the drugs listed above.

Life Insurance Underwriting for Hypertension

To be frank, it is uncommon to see any application of the end-of-life expense company talk about the words high blood pressure or hypertension in their questions about health. In case you don't know if a life insurer does not inquire about a health condition, then they are very okay with it.

Your Expectation When Getting Burial Insurance with High Blood Pressure

Fortunately, if you only have hypertension, you are in a better position to qualify for a funeral insurance plan.

High Blood Pressure is Controllable

We do not know any life insurance company that will reject you for hypertension. You can contact any company, and they will give you immediate protection at the lowest rate.

You Have Had Uncontrolled High Blood Pressure in the Past Two Years

If you found yourself in this category, don't worry. Although there are some (few) companies that do not agree with uncontrolled high blood pressure, there are many that do not care. You will easily be eligible for a level death funeral insurance plan. You would not have a waiting period, and there will not be a need to pay a higher premium. Basically, you will have the same payment as a marathon runner.

How to Get the Best Funeral Insurance for High Blood Pressure

As already mentioned, high blood pressure will in no way complicate your ability to guarantee cheaper insurance for instant funeral expenses. With this, it is extremely simple to find the best life insurance plan with hypertension.

Having a funeral insurance plan is like having a lawyer to help you with your legal issues. You rely on your lawyer to diagnose your case and recommend the best action you should take. Similarly, you need to look at the expertise of an independent end-of-life agency to find out which insurance company will give you the best deal.

Another Thing You Should Consider

This article obviously covers the topic of high blood pressure. In addition, it is important to remember that other health problem that you may encounter, if any, will be included in the equation. As I mentioned, high blood pressure is a problem in almost every company. In addition, you may have other health conditions that could complicate it more.

AL KUSHNER

The Reality of Burial Insurance After Stent Surgery

Trying to get life insurance after heart stent surgery might seem difficult however it doesn't have to be.

High-risk life insurance can sometimes be challenging, but reputable agents like ours have dealt with similar cases couple of times. If you have experienced any blockage in the arteries and need surgery to place stents, you will understand that this is a common procedure. Today, we will take you through how you can simply obtain a life insurance policy if you ever been stent patient as much as possible:

Here are the Main Lessons You Would Learn in this Article

You may take out life insurance after heart stent surgery. As a general rule, if a stent is in place and there are no more problems, you can get life insurance at standard rates after six months of waiting for an application after surgery.

How to Secure Life Insurance After a Stent Surgery

Luckily, various technology available nowadays has afforded human the opportunity to prolong a person's life and help reduce the risk of further heart problems safely and effectively.

All life insurers are well aware of this and will often provide some type of life insurance policy. However, if you have ever been denied a life insurance coverage because you had a stent surgery, then you have a problem.

When it comes to getting life insurance coverage for people that have a stent, expect a life insurance company to assess you like this.

For anyone who has used a stent but has no complications from surgery or other health issues, that person may qualify for standard rates if enough time has elapsed.

The More Time Spent with Constant Monitoring, the Better it Becomes.

Ultimately, it will depend on the individual life insurer and its policies.

If you are an applicant that has more than one stent in place and also has possibly had a heart attack, then you will be eligible for less favorable rates; these are referred to as substandard rates and known as "Table ratings" in our industry.

Again, this will depend on each insurance company and their type of policies.

Some life insurance companies may deny coverage, while others will start with a base table rating, but then ask detailed questions to determine the final rating.

Waiting Six Months Before You Apply for Life Insurance After Stent Surgery

While it is possible to get suitable life insurance coverage, you need to consider a number of factors before applying for life insurance coverage if you have had stent surgery.

All life insurance companies are determined to make you wait for six months before you can apply for life insurance coverage; this is done so that if complications occur as a result of the operation, they will occur within the first six months after the operation. Their policy is always to give time for surgery and physical healing, so they will not process any application before that time.

Underwriting Heart Stents When Applying for Life Insurance

Below are some of the possible question's insurers will ask if you have undergone surgery to put the stent in place:

- How many stents did you have in place?

- Was there anything that led to the need for stents, like a heart attack or stroke?

- What was the result of your last stress test, and when last did you have the test?

- When was the stent put in place?

- What are the medications in your prescription?

- What was the last stress test result and which date did you take the test?

- Have you made any positive lifestyle changes after surgery, such as quitting smoking or starting a fitness plan or fitness regime?

- Have you experienced any chest pains after surgery?

If you cannot provide answers to these questions, you don't have to be scared; we can still provide you an estimate of your rates. However, you have to keep it in mind that it won't be completely accurate.

That being said, without answering these questions about stent surgery, your life insurance agent will not be able to assess your specific risk accurately.

Therefore, be always prepared that if a life insurance agent does not ask you these questions, they will not make an offer that will fully meet your needs.

If you have experienced any chest pain after the stent operation, all insurers will automatically reject your application.

If your stent surgery was performed over five years ago without complications or additional treatment, you might get life insurance that does not need you to undergo a medical exam.

The best procedure to search for suitable and affordable life insurance for any applicants having these types of health problems, such as someone who needs diabetes life insurance quotes, is to look for an independent consultant who can understand the perceptions of each life insurers.

If you have ever been denied a life insurance coverage before, but do not understand why it might mean you are looking in the wrong place.

We are always turning declines into having a life insurance coverage as we are specialist at dealing with higher risk.

If you are currently having heart problems or even serious health complications, reach out to us, and we will check with all our life insurers to find the best deal for you.

Guaranteed Life Insurance is Available for Any Stent Patient

Also, we have graded death benefit policies that are available at highly competitive rates, which ensures that most of our clients have some type of life insurance coverage.

These plans make medical underwriting easier, which further makes getting approval simple.

There is a waiting period of 2 years, which starts as soon as you sign the insurance plan documents.

If you pass away in the first two years of the policy, your family will not be entitled for an. Instead, they will receive a refund of the premiums you have paid up to that point.

Here's one way in which the insurer can even up with the risk of your surgery.

After the two years waiting period, your policy will work as a traditional insurance policy.

Collaborate with an agency like ours to get life insurance if you have had a Heart Stent Surgery.

Getting Life Insurance After Undergoing Heart Stent Surgery Does Not Have to Come with Complications

As an agency, our sole aim is to offer a comprehensive and extensive service to our potential clients and strive to build a relationship with you based on our understanding of your individual needs.

Our life insurance agents are made up of highly qualified consultants who will discuss your needs and assess the level of insurance coverage you need putting into consideration the stents and adapted according to your personal lifestyle.

We are always confident that we can find all life insurance options suitable for our clients, which are specifically tailored to suits their needs and offer the highest level of insurance coverage at the best price possible.

Our agents have many years of experience helping applicants tagged as being "High risk" to obtain the coverage they need, and this, beyond doubt, includes applicants who have recently have stent surgery.

It does not matter whether you have been refused life insurance coverage before; it should not make you conclude that you wouldn't qualify for insurance coverage. Irrespective of your health or other conditions, there are many available quality options you can get.

Do not delay again before you obtain a life insurance coverage; reach out to one of our agents, and we would be excited to get you started.

Elite Guide to Buying Burial Insurance with a Bundle Branch Block

Insurance with a pre-existing condition is never easy, especially when that is bundle branch block. This article is to help you understand your options for this process.

To guarantee that you receive the most beneficial and most affordable insurance policy, we will use our years of experience helping people with Bundle Branch Blocks (BBB). Here are some of the topics we will cover:

- How Bundle Branch Block and Heart Block Impact Life Insurance Coverage

- What to Expect When Purchasing Life Insurance with Bundle Branch Block

- Purchasing Other Types of Insurance with Bundle Branch Block

- How We Can Help You Secure Coverage with Bundle Branch Block

What Are the Fundamental Details to Take Away from this Article?

Getting life insurance with bundle branch block should not be a problem. The primary details that will be considered for coverage approval will be the length of time you have had bundle branch block and any other additional health conditions commonly present with it.

How Bundle Branch Block and Heart Block Impact Life Insurance Coverage

The most common cause of BBB, about 50 percent of all cases, is coronary artery disease. Additional conditions that could cause this illness include cardiomyopathy, hypertension, tumors, fibrosis of the conduction fibers, congenital lesions, trauma, and aortic stenosis. That being said, a heart that has no apparent ailments may also get BBB. Underlying causes will be taken into account by the underwriters assisting you with life insurance coverage.

For us to find the most accurate policy for your situation, we will want to know some of the following information from you:

- The type of bundle branch block that you have

- How long you have been diagnosed with bundle branch block

- If any new developments have been noticed on an ECG

- If you have been diagnosed with angina, cardiomyopathy, hypertension, congenital heart disease, or valvular heart disease

- If you have completed any cardiac studies

- What medications you take

We will need as much information as reasonable to find the best, most affordable coverage for you for all of the above-listed items. We are looking out for you, so it is vital to provide as upfront and accurate as possible with this information.

It is understandable if you do not possess all of the specifics, though. Underwriters can fill in those gaps when they do a deep dive into your medical history. While they take care of that, we can still provide an estimation of the coverage cost.

What to Expect When Purchasing Life Insurance with Bundle Branch Block

When you start the process of shopping for life insurance with BBB, you should make sure that you possess a firm understanding of your medical history as it applies to the diagnosis. The entirety of your medical records is not necessary, but you should at least have a detailed timeline of your BBB diagnosis. Currently, you will have to have a medical exam to obtain life insurance from the type of insurance companies you will want to look at, companies that offer fully underwritten policies.

Also, your BBB status will likely cause your costs to be higher than that of the average healthy person. This is entirely dependent on your situation, meaning that they can be slightly higher or significantly higher. A little later in this piece, we will be discussing some of the specific ratings that can be presumed for life insurance with BBB.

To summarize, though one of our talented high-risk life insurance agents can help, getting life insurance with BBB is a complicated process. It will be best to come to the table with as much detail as you can. Do not forget that you are shopping for coverage. It is okay to gather offers from multiple life insurance companies before choosing to get the most affordable coverage. Companies need your business so that they will fight for it.

So, to speed up that shopping process, make sure, again, to come as prepared as possible. Understand that the life insurance underwriters may require more details and may involve gathering specific medical records or having your primary care physician produce more information.

The Life Insurance with Bundle Branch Block Underwriting Process

Suppose you have no known heart disease, and your BBB was from an isolated finding. In that case, you will get a standard life insurance valuation, assuming your ECG history does not include pattern changes involving:

- Incomplete Right Bundle Branch Block (IRBBB)

- Complete Right Bundle Branch Block (CRBBB) - not including Sarcoidosis

- Left Anterior or Posterior Hemiblock (LAHB or LPHB)

Nevertheless, your policy cost will be higher, starting at Table B, if you have a complete Left or Right Bundle Branch Block. It can also be higher if you have additional conditions. But if you have a recent, healthy thallium stress test, have had no other cardiovascular impairments, and have been stable for at least six years, then you will be able to get standard rates.

There are no term life insurance carriers that do not require a medical exam if you have BBB, but if you are over 50 with BBB, limited-term life insurance does not need a medical exam. Taking a medical exam is unavoidable for term life insurance coverage.

Working with a trusted life insurance agent is paramount. With the experience that we have with working with those that have had a diagnosis of bundle branch block, or heart problems in general, we can accurately assess your specific risk to find the best available coverage for you.

Purchasing Other Types of Insurance with Bundle Branch Block

It is important to note that there is always a possibility of getting denied insurance coverage with any health condition. Cases deemed high-risk, especially those in which the individual has health problems in addition to the BBB, may struggle to find affordable rates or even get approved at all. It is for this reason why you should look to reputable agencies that specialize in these cases.

If you are refused coverage or offered a far from affordable policy, other options to consider are guaranteed life insurance or accidental death life insurance. You will not be required to take a medical exam for these other types of policies, but the coverage you receive will be far less than a regular life insurance plan and will have additional requirements.

How We Can Help You Secure Coverage with Bundle Branch Block

Our ample amount of experience dealing with this high-risk condition allows us to be in the best place possible to help you get the lowest available rates on your life insurance policy. With the ability to work with over 60 life insurance companies, Superior Mutual has the knowledge and ability to navigate the market for you.

If your bundle branch block is mild, head on over to our instant rate form and select "regular to see a selection of instant quotes. Otherwise, call us at Superior Mutual, and we can work with you and your situation to find your best life insurance policy.

The Reality of Burial Insurance with Cholesterol Medication

Are you taking medication for high cholesterol and are searching for burial insurance? If so, do you know what affects cholesterol medication will have when you apply?

Here's the Truth.

Affordable burial insurance is not hard to find. No, really, not even if you take cholesterol medication. We have worked with countless customers who take cholesterol medication. We did it for them; we can do it for you. This article will demonstrate what the underwriting policy is and how to get the best coverage. If you finish reading this and still have questions, let us know. We are here to help you.

The Scoop on Burial Insurance and Cholesterol Medication

It might come as a surprise, but final expense life insurance companies are unconcerned about high cholesterol. You won't have an issue finding quality insurance.

So, What's the Bottom Line?

Burial insurance applications do have questions about cholesterol issues, or the medications associated with them. A person with excellent health will pay the same rate as you. As if that's not good enough, there will be no coverage waiting period.

No Physical or Medical Exam is Required for Burial Insurance

It's not a hidden fact that high cholesterol increases the chance of stroke or heart problems. But merely managing your LDL levels is a complete nonissue when applying for burial insurance.

High Cholesterol Underwriting

Essentially, there is none. It's as transparent as that. Insurance companies don't ask about high cholesterol on burial applications. Moreover, all medications are accepted. Even if you are taking multiple high cholesterol medications, it will not be an issue. Remember, if it is not on the burial insurance application, it won't affect the policy.

By now, you have probably soaked in the information that securing burial insurance is not a laborious process if you are taking cholesterol medication. However, if you have any other health issues, be aware that they will factor in the underwriting process. Final expense life insurance companies will ask various questions depending on their coverage policies. It is essential to know this. Just because high cholesterol is acceptable under their system doesn't mean other health conditions are.

What's the Bottom Line Here?

It is of extreme importance to be upfront about all of your health conditions. We need to know everything to thoroughly assess your situation and determine which insurance carriers will be most appropriate for you.

A Step by Step Guide to Burial Insurance with a Blood Clot

If you have recently had a blood clot, you may want to know how it affects the price and coverage of funeral insurance. In fact, many of our clients who experienced blood clots started asking these questions directly.

Blood clots usually appear to have little or no effect. We often help many clients with blood clots secure affordable life insurance for final expenses, and we can also help you. We will let you know how we assisted them so that you know what to expect.

This article will cover how blood clots can affect funeral insurance prices, how insurers react to this health condition, and how you can get the full policy at the lowest cost.

The Reality of Burial Insurance After a Blood Clot

Some burial insurance companies will inquire about blood clots, but most do not. All of this means that in the vast majority of cases, blood clots are not actually a problem.

To buy funeral insurance after a blood clot, you are more likely to qualify for simplified or level death benefits. This is also applicable if you have had a pulmonary embolism. And this means you will be entitled to a policy that has full protection from the first day, and your payment would be the lowest offered by insurers. Generally, you would have to pay more for a blood clot or go through a waiting period if you should have some form of surgery to fix it (which is uncommon)

Here is the Conclusion

Some insurers are concerned about blood clots, and others are not. Because we have access to several companies, we would only give you access to one of the funeral insurance companies that would not care about blood cloth.

Oh, and see this ...

No funeral insurance plan will require you to undergo a physical or medical examination as part of your application. The main thing you will do is answer some questions about your health.

Burial Insurance Underwriting for Blood Clots

In most situation, underwriting blood clots focus more on treatment. It is true that some insurers ask you about blood clots and penalizes you for it. However, this is really unusual. Most burial insurance companies will not inquire about blood clots. Just because it doesn't question them means they are not concerned about it.

In order to be able to state accurately and provide a clear and predictable result, we will ask some questions about blood clots.

- When was your last diagnosis for blood clots?

- Did you undergo any surgery for blood clot treatment?

- Did you take any medications? If yes, when were they prescribed?

- Did you ever have a diagnosis for Deep Vein Thrombosis?

- Do you have other health problems? If yes, did you treat it?

After knowing this information, we can tell you precisely the company that will offer you the best option and what they will charge exactly.

Let's be Clear About a Few Things

If you had experienced pulmonary embolism or have diagnosis for deep vein thrombosis, there won't be a problem for you qualifying for a level death benefit of many insurers. We have many end-of-life insurance companies with underwriting that will accept you wholeheartedly without problems.

Read below to find out how the end-of-life companies will respond to potential cases of blood clotting.

Medications

There may be several medications prescribed when the doctor finds a blood clot. In most situations, antidepressants like Coumadin, Eliquis, Xarelto are usually the first type of treatment. However, the great news is that there are many funeral insurers that agree perfectly with or blood thinners. You will still be entitled to death benefits.

Surgery

Although very unusual, surgery may sometimes be necessary to treat blood clots, deep vein thrombosis and pulmonary embolism. The commonest is installing a Vena Cava filter. Irrespective of the surgery type, if you perform any type of surgery on any part of the circulatory system, it will greatly affect your coverage.

The Way Insurance Company Offer Policies Depend on the Time of Surgery

You have had surgery in the last 12 months.

Most end-of-life insurers will only offer policies with higher payment rates (15-30% more), with a waiting period of two years. And this is a guaranteed acceptance policy.

You have had surgery in the last 12 months, but only in the last 24 months.

Most of the top-rated insurers we will offer you will only check as far as 12 months for blood clot surgery applicants.

If you have had no problems beyond the blood-clotting operation in the past 24 months, we will likely find a simplified type of end-of-life insurance policy, which means lower payment rates and instant insurance coverage (no waiting period)

If surgery took place 24 months ago

In this situation, most of our best insurance companies will practically disregard that you undergo blood clot surgery if it was more than 24 months ago. You are sure to find a simplified or level type of insurance for final expenses with instant first-day insurance coverage.

The Secret to Getting Burial Insurance on Blood Thinners

There is a very fearful misconception that finding burial insurance on blood thinners is an impossible task.

We know better.

It is within reach for everyone to find affordable burial insurance on blood thinners. It comes as no surprise there is a "higher risk" stigma attached to taking blood thinners. But this does not mean you are obstructed from qualifying for affordable coverage.

We can help you find your solution. We know how possible it is to find a quality insurance plan that treats you the same way they'd treat an Olympic athlete.

Take into account there is not a medical exam you will encounter while qualifying for final life insurance. Insurance companies will not need access to doctor's records or other tests when assessing you for coverage. They will ask your health questions for the best policy fit.

Let's walk through the necessary steps of qualifying for burial insurance while taking blood thinners.

Underwriting Process

The underwriting process is to see where you are on the risk scale. It's the process of answering a few medical questions. In most cases, the words "blood thinner" are not even seen on the application. Sounds strange, right? Well, it's not that strange. Insurance companies have a medication list. The funeral insurance companies have flagged medications on that list. Those flagged medications so happen to be blood-thinning. See where I'm going with this?

Every insurer then responds in their way. They can categorize those who take certain blood thinners into higher-risk categories or not.

Time is also an influence in the underwriting process. Medication lists will vary depending on how long you've been on certain medications. Insurance companies will be able to see this information.

Some final expense policies have a "first fill" protocol. This means that your policy coverage might change depending on how long it's been since your first prescription fill. In most cases, if two years have passed since your first fill, most insurance companies will view you as a lower risk. On the other hand, if you first filled your prescription within the last two years, you might be at higher risk. Every insurance company is different and responds to blood thinners in their own way.

Remember, we have companies we represent who remain neutral about blood thinner medications, even if you've been prescribed recently. Let us help you set your future self-up for success. We are here for you, and we don't want you to face a penalty for taking care of your health.

Below is a list of popular blood thinners that burial insurance companies look out for:

- Apixaban (Eliquis)
- Aspirin
- Clopidogrel (Plavix)
- Dabigatran (Pradaxa)
- Dipyridamole (Persantine)

- Edoxaban (Savaysa)
- Fondaparinux (Arixtra)
- Heparin
- Plavix (Clopidogrel)
- Prasugrel (Effient)
- Rivaroxaban (Xarelto)
- Ticagrelor (Brilinta)
- Ticlid (Ticlopidine)
- Vorapaxar (Zontivity)
- Warfarin (Coumadin)

Here are some common ways insurance companies could respond to blood thinner medication:

- **They require a higher monthly payment.**

This response is straightforward. You take blood thinners; you receive a higher premium payment. Insurance companies see this as a way to offset the increased risk they view blood thinners as. You are still covered in full starting day one.

- **They require a higher premium and impose a waiting period.**

With this response, expect to pay 40-60% more than someone who is considered in perfect health. Also, your benefits will not payout during the first two years unless your death is ruled accidental.

- **They require a higher premium and limit payout of benefit within the first two years.**

With this response, expect to pay around 15-30% more than someone who is considered in perfect health. Death benefits pay out within two years. This is usually divided into 30% payout the first year and 70% payout the second year. This is a pretty uncommon action among insurance companies.

- **There is no policy change because blood thinners are not assessed as high risk.**

With this response, expect to pay the same price as someone who is considered in perfect health. These insurance companies treat blood thinners as a trivial matter in the grand scheme of health. You are covered in full starting on day one.

Questions to Expect from Us

We strive to connect you with the best carrier possible. You are our focus; finding the best possible solution is our responsibility. If you are searching for immediate benefits while looking to avoid long wait times, let us help you. To help you, we must know you. Here are some questions about blood thinners you can expect us to ask:

- What blood thinners do you take presently?

- What date was your prescription first filled for the blood thinner(s)?

- Why are you taking these presently?

- Have you ever not filled your prescription and refilled again within the last two years?

- Have you consistently filled the prescription regularly since you were first prescribed it?

We will also ask about any other underlying health issues and medical information. We analyze your entire health profile and match you with a carrier that will give you the excellent coverage for your health.

When we have all the information, we can connect you to carriers with low rates and compassionate coverage.

Getting Burial Insurance When You are Living with a Pacemaker

You've always provided for your family as well as you could. You would like that to stay the same even if you were to pass away.

Funerals are expensive nowadays, no matter what style you choose. And of course, all the regular expenses of life still go on. Your family doesn't need more stress while they're grieving.

So, you are considering getting burial and life insurance but there's a catch...

You are one of the 3 million people currently living with a pacemaker worldwide.

You might be worrying if you can even get burial insurance or life insurance with a pacemaker. If they do insure you, what will the rates be like?

First, let us calm your fears.

Yes, you absolutely can obtain insurance even if you have a pacemaker.

Now the process might be a little different and it will affect the rates with some companies.

But there's no need to worry because we're breaking down everything you need to know about obtaining burial or life insurance when you have a pacemaker.

What Is a Pacemaker

A pacemaker is a tiny electronic device that gets implanted in your chest. It stimulates your heart to beat at the correct rate.

A pacemaker might be needed to treat conditions where the heart either beats too fast or too slow. These can include, but aren't limited to:

- After a heart attack
- Heart block
- Sick Sinus Syndrome
- Heart failure
- Bradycardia

Installing a pacemaker is actually a fairly minor surgery. A surgeon will make a small incision in the chest then thread a noodle-like wire through a vein into the heart. This monitors the heart rhythm.

The surgeon confirms the leads are in the right place and then connects them to a battery-powered generator. The device is then programmed to get your heartbeat to the correct rate. Once that is adjusted, the pacemaker is inserted into a small pocket underneath your collarbone.

You will likely stay in the hospital overnight just so the healthcare team can make sure the pacemaker is working but after that much of your follow up is done remotely.

A pacemaker insertion does qualify as a heart or circulatory surgery and we'll talk more about why this is important later.

The Type of Pacemaker That You Have Usually Doesn't Matter

Pacemakers come in two varieties, single chamber and dual chamber.

A single-chamber pacemaker uses one wire in either the upper chamber or the lower chamber of the right side of the heart.

A dual-chamber pacemaker has one wire in the right upper chamber and one lead in the right lower chamber of your heart.

Insurance companies do not differentiate between these two types of pacemakers. In fact, it's highly unlikely that any insurance company will ask you which type you have.

So this isn't something that you need to worry about.

How Long Ago Your Pacemaker Was Implanted Does

In general, just having a pacemaker isn't considered a major risk factor by final expense or life insurance companies. But how long ago it was put in is one factor that will have some influence on the underwriting process.

The amount of time that has elapsed since your pacemaker was implanted will affect your premiums and any potential waiting periods for full coverage.

We'll break this down in detail in the rate discussion section below.

What About Battery Changes?

Pacemaker batteries last anywhere from 5-15 years, but on average need to be changed every 6-7 years. Pacemaker battery changes are considered a minor outpatient procedure. You likely won't even stay in the hospital overnight unless you have other medical conditions.

Some burial and life insurance companies will consider a pacemaker battery change as a heart or circulatory system surgery while others will not.

This makes choosing the correct broker very important. An experienced insurance broker will know which insurance companies view a pacemaker battery change as surgery and can direct you to the ones that don't.

The Insurance Application Process

People with pacemakers are rarely declined for insurance as long as their other health conditionals are stabilized.

The application process for burial insurance or life insurance can vary slightly from company to company, but here's what you can generally expect.

All types of insurance companies will ask you about your tobacco use history, alcohol use, and drug use.

Insurance companies will also review your prescription medications. From this list, they can get an idea of what illnesses you have now or in the past from the medications that were prescribed to treat them.

Health Questions About Your Pacemaker

While an insurance company may or may not specifically ask about a pacemaker, they will ask you about and recent heart or circulatory surgeries. As mentioned previously, having a pacemaker inserted does qualify as a surgery.

The good news is that there is also usually a timeframe specified in the question. 12 months or 24 months are the most common.

If your surgery or most recent generator battery change were outside of the window specified in the question, you can truthfully answer this question "No".

The most important thing is to just be honest. Again, it is unlikely for you to be completely declined for life or burial insurance based on the presence of a pacemaker alone.

Will They Ask for Medical Records?

Most companies do not request your medical records, although in some instances it might actually be beneficial for you to provide some.

The underwriter will mostly be concerned with your underlying medical conditions (including the one that needed a pacemaker), how they affect your health, and how well your doctor has treated them.

These conditions will affect your rates but will not likely stop you from obtaining insurance.

What Can I Expect for Rates and Waiting Periods?

As mentioned above, the amount of time since your pacemaker was placed will be the biggest factor in determining your rates for burial insurance or life insurance.

You likely will be considered at higher risk for insurance purposes, but this should not stop you from applying.

Now, its a little tricky to pinpoint the actual costs. The amount of insurance coverage, type, and duration will all play a part. This is true even for someone without a pacemaker.

But, in general, this is what you can expect if you fall into the following categories.

My Doctor Just Told Me That I Need a Pacemaker

If your cardiologist just told you that you need a pacemaker or you are currently in the hospital waiting to have one implanted, you likely will have to wait for a short period of time to apply.

One the pacemaker insertion is complete, and you've had a few follow-up appointments, you'll fall into the category below.

My Pacemaker Was Put in Less Than 12 Months Ago

If your pacemaker was implanted less than a year ago you can still get life or final expense insurance, but you will have to pay a slightly increased premium (most commonly 15-30% more).

You might also have a 2-year waiting period. If you pass away within this period, the insurance company will refund your premium with some interest and pay this out to your beneficiaries. After the two years, you will have regular coverage.

While the increased premiums and waiting period can't be avoided, an experienced insurance agency can have your situation reevaluated when you reach the 1-year mark. You may be able to apply for a lower rate and full coverage without the waiting period at that time.

I've Had My Pacemaker for More Than 12 Months

Now, most underwriting companies will look back 2 years when asking you about your health conditions. But there are some burial and life insurance companies that only look back 1 year.

An expert insurance agent will be able to direct you to them.

If you are asked about heart or circulatory system surgeries in the last 12 months, you can honestly say "no". Barring other health issues, you could expect normal rates and instant coverage.

Even if you do have to disclose your pacemaker surgery, the increased premiums and waiting period won't be as long. And your agent can reevaluate when you hit the 2-year mark.

It's Been More Than 24 Months Since My Pacemaker Was Put in

Congratulations, you are most likely free and clear on the pacemaker issue.

All but the strictest life insurance or burial insurance companies will offer you their standard rates. And the ones that won't are a small minority your agent can help you avoid.

You should be able to obtain insurance with immediate coverage and the smallest premium that is available.

In Conclusion

Don't let having a pacemaker stop you from applying for burial insurance or life insurance.

You can get affordable rates and terms even if you are living with a pacemaker.

Choosing the right insurance broker to work with is key.

An experienced insurance agent will have worked with many carriers over the years and helped multiple people in your exact same situation.

Contact us today and let us help you find the best company to meet your insurance needs.

Surefire Way to Get Burial Insurance with Dialysis

Lately, it's no news, neither is it surprising that when on dialysis, getting life insurance is close to almost impossible. While this might be the truth in most cases, being on dialysis takes you out or reduces your chances of qualifying for the traditional life insurance, that's a different story for burial insurance.

Yeah, you read that right, burial insurance.

Even when you are on a dialysis for a failing kidney, you can still get a new burial insurance policy.

At Superior Mutual, we have adequate experience in helping people with renal diseases who are going through dialysis. We had the option to support them, and today we will show you precisely how you can meet all requirements for the most affordable burial insurance policy conceivable.

In this article, you will figure out how burial insurance companies respond to dialysis candidates, what reasonable choices you will have, and how you can locate the most awesome funeral policy.

Here's the Truth about Burial Insurance on Dialysis

If it's not too much trouble, you should be careful of what you read online on this topic. We realize that most clients will explore numerous sites before settling on a consensus. We are here to present to you the brutal truth since we would prefer not to delude you. Mind you, a lot of things you read online as regards burial insurance on dialysis is very wrong.

Most importantly, you can get a policy even as you are on your dialysis. Nonetheless, the thing you should know and acknowledge is that no life insurance company on the planet will provide you with a policy that protects you at all during the first 24 months. Being on dialysis implies you should wait this 24 months before the insurer pays out a death claim. Should you somehow happened to pass during the initial two years, the insurer would discount all the charges you have ever paid in addition to interest.

We know and comprehend that it's disappointing to find out that it's difficult to get coverage that secures you in any form during the initial two years. We employ you not to think we are making this up. Like we referenced, the main objective is to bring you the real truth.

Be sure to leave here with the notion that you just need to look for a company that will cover you quickly, however, you will be searching forever to achieve that. You won't find it anywhere.

Why There Is a Need to Wait as a Dialysis Patient

The reality of this circumstance is that individuals on dialysis have an essentially lower life expectancy than normal individuals. This is the reason no company will give you coverage without a holding up time of at least two years.

Luckily, following your physician's instructions and diligently taking your dialysis medicines can prolong your life for numerous years. Without a doubt, you are on a transfer list, so we trust and implore that one day a donor will come through for you. As a result, burial insurance is still truly available to you. It's simply going to have the previously mentioned waiting up period.

How Final Expense Companies Underwrite Dialysis

The vast majority know about the term endorsing or underwriting. It is just how the insurance company determines the level of your risk level to assess eligibility. Companies offering burial insurance will make an inquiry regarding your health and investigate your prescription history to underwrite your application.

Despite how they discover it, burial life insurance companies have two reactions to candidates on dialysis.

1. They deny you coverage out and out.

2. They offer you an arrangement with at least a long-term waiting period alongside a lot higher month to month premium. Most insurers will get some information about dialysis in the following ways, or something as the same as this:

Have you ever gotten or been encouraged to get kidney dialysis?

A few companies may attach a particular timeframe to their inquiry like this:

Within the last 1 year, have you ever gotten or been encouraged to get kidney dialysis?

Regardless of how the information was received, you can't deny the fact that dialysis will create your one and only option.

How to Get Burial Insurance While on Dialysis

When going through current dialysis treatment, your only choice to secure another burial policy is to take out what's known as a guaranteed issue life insurance policy. There are no health questions on these types of policies. Moreover, they don't check your clinical history in any way.

Be that as it may, here's the kicker with these. Regardless of what insurance company gives a guaranteed acceptance life policy, there are some general facts you have to think about them.

1. There will be at least a two-year holding up period. There are a couple of life insurance companies that require 3 years; however, they are rare.

2. The month-to-month charge will be higher than a burial insurance plan where you deny all its health questions.

The Ideal Option for Acute Kidney Failure Patients

Acute kidney failure is significantly more unprecedented than kidney failure because of stage 5 chronic kidney disease. The fundamental distinction with acute kidney failure is that the dialysis therapy is temporary. When your kidneys recover, you will not need dialysis anymore. This entire situation is very different from somebody with end-stage renal failure which requires dialysis. If this is your condition, this is what you do:

Stage 1) immediately take out a guaranteed issue policy.

Stage 2) once you have a year added to you since your last dialysis treatment, you can apply for a burial insurance plan with a carrier where some information is received about dialysis within one year. Since it's been longer than a year, you could state no. You would easily qualify for a policy that provides immediate coverage which will cost you way less.

The Best No Health Question Policy

Now, you know which type of policy is your lone alternative. The main outstanding question is which company offers the best arrangement on a guaranteed issue policy? Before we bounce into that, we must make something properly understood. The best-guaranteed acceptance life insurance policy is just the less expensive, and it just has a 2-year waiting period.

Utilizing that equation as a benchmark, there are just two life insurance companies that meet those prerequisites. Beyond a shadow of a doubt, there are many companies available today that offer these plans.

Today, the two we show you are by a wide margin indisputably the least expensive companies out of all. These two companies are almost the same in cost. They usually differ by less than a dollar.

Sons of Norway Guaranteed Acceptance Burial Insurance

- Age Limits: 0-85

- Face Amount Limits: $5,000-$25,000

- State Availability: All states except CA or NY (We have Gerber Life for CA/NY)

Sons of Norway is a great company, and we do represent them. If you are looking to get a policy with them, call us at 1-888-810-9725

Sons of Norway Male Rates

AGE	$5,000	$10,000	$15,000	$20,000
50	$18.30	$36.59	$54.89	$73.19
51	$19.19	$38.39	$57.58	$76.77
52	$20.15	$40.30	$60.45	$80.60
53	$21.17	$42.34	$63.51	$84.68
54	$22.25	$44.51	$66.76	$89.01

AGE	$5,000	$10,000	$15,000	$20,000
55	$23.41	$46.83	$70.24	$93.65
56	$24.41	$48.42	$73.24	$97.65
57	$25.47	$50.94	$76.41	$101.88
58	$26.60	$53.19	$79.79	$107.39
59	$27.78	$55.56	$83.35	$111.13
60	$29.04	$58.09	$87.13	$116.18
61	$30.19	$60.38	$90.56	$120.75
62	$31.39	$62.79	$94.18	$125.58
63	$32.66	$65.32	$97.98	$130.65
64	$34.00	$67.99	$101.99	$135.98
65	$35.41	$70.82	$106.23	$141.64
66	$37.12	$74.23	$111.13	$148.46
67	$38.94	$77.89	$116.83	$155.77
68	$40.91	$81.82	$122.73	$163.64

AGE	**$5,000**	**$10,000**	**$15,000**	**$20,000**
69	$43.02	$86.05	$129.07	$172.09
70	$45.29	$90.58	$135.88	$181.17
71	$47.46	$94.92	$142.38	$189.84
72	$49.77	$99.54	$149.30	$199.07
73	$52.22	$104.45	$156.67	$208.90
74	$54.83	$109.67	$164.50	$219.33
75	$57.63	$115.25	$172.88	$230.50
76	$59.82	$119.64	$179.46	$239.28
77	$62.13	$124.26	$186.39	$248.52
78	$64.58	$129.17	$193.75	$258.33
79	$67.18	$134.36	$201.54	$275.55
80	$69.93	$139.85	$209.78	$268.72
81	$75.86	$151.72	$227.57	$303.43
82	$82.45	$164.89	$247.34	$329.78

AGE	$5,000	$10,000	$15,000	$20,000
83	$89.72	$179.44	$269.15	$358.87
84	$97.71	$195.42	$293.14	$390.85
85	$106.44	$212.88	$319.32	$425.77

Sons of Norway Female Rates

AGE	$5,000	$10,000	$15,000	$20,000
50	$13.81	$27.63	$41.44	$55.25
51	$14.38	$28.76	$43.15	$57.53
52	$14.98	$29.95	$44.93	$59.91
53	$15.61	$31.22	$46.83	$62.44
54	$16.27	$32.55	$48.82	$65.09
55	$16.98	$33.96	$50.94	$67.92
56	$17.62	$35.24	$52.86	$70.48
57	$18.29	$36.58	$54.88	$73.17

AGE	$5,000	$10,000	$15,000	$20,000
58	$19.00	$38.00	$57.01	$76.04
59	$19.75	$39.50	$59.25	$79.00
60	$20.54	$41.07	$61.61	$82.14
61	$21.28	$42.57	$63.85	$85.14
62	$22.07	$44.14	$66.21	$88.28
63	$22.89	$45.79	$68.68	$91.58
64	$23.76	$47.52	$71.27	$95.03
65	$24.67	$49.33	$74.00	$98.67
66	$25.89	$51.77	$77.66	$103.55
67	$27.19	$54.38	$81.57	$147.58
68	$28.58	$57.16	$85.74	$108.77
69	$30.07	$60.14	$90.21	$114.33
70	$31.66	$63.33	$94.99	$120.28
71	$33.35	$66.99	$100.04	$133.38

AGE	$5,000	$10,000	$15,000	$20,000
72	$35.16	$70.33	$105.49	$140.66
73	$37.12	$74.25	$111.37	$148.50
74	$39.25	$78.50	$117.75	$157.00
75	$41.55	$83.10	$124.64	$166.19
76	$43.57	$87.14	$130.71	$174.24
77	$45.75	$91.49	$137.24	$182.99
78	$48.09	$96.18	$144.27	$192.36
79	$50.62	$101.24	$151.85	$202.47
80	$53.33	$106.27	$160.00	$213.33
81	$57.63	$115.25	$172.88	$230.50
82	$62.35	$124.70	$187.04	$249.39
83	$67.53	$135.06	$202.60	$270.13
84	$73.21	$146.42	$219.63	$292.84
85	$79.39	$158.79	$238.18	$317.58

The Golden Rule with Respect to the Ensured Issue of Life Insurance

We have made it painfully certain that individuals with kidney failure requiring dialysis can just get a guaranteed issue plan. Notwithstanding, if that isn't your circumstance, you don't need a guaranteed issue policy until you thoroughly investigate different alternatives.

Here's the main concern.

Here is a straightforward principle to follow concerning no health question policies:

You should just apply for a no-health question policy once you determine for sure that you can't qualify for a plan where you would say NO to all the health questions (or the greater part of them). Then it would help if you resorted to a guaranteed issue policy. By far, most of the individuals we are in communication with can and do qualify for insurance that has health-related questions. Indeed, we can find a policy for 90% of our customers whose coverage secures them in full right away.

The lesson of the story

If you're not on dialysis, call us first to discover what your most ideal alternatives are. We will offer it to you straight. Almost certainly, a guaranteed issue plan won't be your best and least expensive decision available.

Step by Step Instructions to Buying the Best Burial Insurance on Dialysis

If you are suffering from end-stage renal failure, then you should go with Gerber Life, Sons of Norway or Mutual of Omaha. This is truly clear now. Nonetheless, if you are looking for burial insurance for another person who isn't on dialysis, you can follow a basic formula to guarantee you locate the best plan.

To locate the best burial insurance, you should talk with a seasoned free burial insurance office representing lots of insurance companies. Only an independent agency (like Superior Mutual) can pull cites from different insurance companies to determine the one that offers the lowest cost on your burial plan.

We earnestly hope you offer us the chance to earn your business. However, we realize that it will not be the case for everyone. If you decide to go somewhere else, make sure they have loads of carriers they work with. Also, they should be knowledgeable about how final expenses companies react to a health condition.

However long you utilize that as a prerequisite, you are in good hands. If you would like to get some help with no obligation, call us at 1-888-810- 9725.

Burial insurance with Cystic Fibrosis - A Complete Breakdown

This situation can develop in many ways, depending on how severe your case is.

Eventually, most people with cystic fibrosis can fully qualify for coverage that covers them immediately. In addition, their plan won't be so costlier than what a normal person can pay for. In contrast, there are some situations in which you may have to pay more and/or suffer a waiting period; however, it is uncommon.

Here is the good news.

You only have to answer certain questions regarding your health when applying. You don't have to go through a physical or medical examination. An outsider will not need to enter your home to fill out the form.

Living with cystic fibrosis is not easy. Regular mucus removal and breathing problems can be continuously exhausting. We are pleased to tell you that your condition might not have any effect on the premium or policy.

Can Someone with Cystic Fibrosis Obtain Life Insurance?

With current medical advances, people who are prone to CF have a very high chance of exceeding age limits of survivability.

Most Top-rated funeral insurers who receive CF candidates know that people with cystic fibrosis can have a happy life with regular treatment, taking preventive measures, and a good lifestyle.

For these reasons, candidates with cystic fibrosis can be offered the cheapest funeral plan or end of life expense insurance and immediate insurance coverage from day one, which does not include a waiting period.

Insurers usually refer to these plans as Simplified, preferred, or level. One of the best things is that you would never undergo a medical or physical examination.

However,

On the other hand, there are common CF conflicts that can have a negative impact on the insurance policies offered to you.

There are some funeral insurance companies that cite or describe CF in their questions during underwriting, which means you have to answer in the affirmative. It could simply mean that they do not have a low-cost insurance plan for people with CF, or that they will reject the application.

CF greatly affects the airways of the lungs, so some bronchodilators, which are also used for chronic bronchitis and COPD emphysema, can categorize you as being high-risk.

If your doctor has indicated that you still have access to oxygen or need a transplant of the lung, you certainly cannot get simplified coverage.

In general, the quality and potential price of insurance plans that may be offered to you depend on how severe your CF is.

So, how do you qualify for a simplified or level insurance policy? You must complete an underwriting process.

Cystic Fibrosis Underwriting

Underwriting is a risk assessment process. Each funeral insurer will use two procedures to make you qualified for insurance.

- You will be questioned about your health.

- They will go through your prescription history.

These two questions will together provide the insurer information it needs to determine your eligibility.

Health Questions

To be honest, you rarely find a life insurer questioning you directly about cystic fibrosis.

If you find a company asking about CF, the questions will be similar to this.

- Have you ever been diagnosed or treated for cystic fibrosis?

Also, expect questions like this:

- Have you ever received treatment for any severe lung conditions?

The question above will commonly refer to conditions like chronic bronchitis, COPD. Nevertheless, some burial insurance companies consider CF as a severe lung condition.

Medications and Treatment History Evaluation of Cystic Fibrosis

This is essentially an additional effort of insurance companies striving to find out serious health problems that have not been properly or truly dealt with in the underwriting process.

By making use of computer programs, they can easily analyze prescription history. They will know all the prescriptions you have received, and they will know about the medicines prescribed to you - they will know the illnesses you have or being treated for.

As for the insurer, if you are given a prescription for a disease, then you have it.

Below are the types of cystic fibrosis medicines

- Antibiotics for the lungs

- Anti-inflammatory medications for lung airways

- Bronchodilators

- Mucus thinning drugs

Oral pancreatic enzymes to better absorb nutrients from the digestive system.

The only medication among the ones listed above that can cause some problems are bronchodilators, as they are also used for some COPD like chronic bronchitis and emphysema, as well as asthma.

Specific Medications for Cystic Fibrosis

Below are some of the specific medications for treating cystic fibrosis. If you fill out a prescription for any of these drugs, automatically, you will be considered as a CF patient.

- Elexacaftor

- Dornase Alfa

- Ivacaftor

- Lumacaftor

- Orkambi

- Tezacaftor

Some other treatments are

- Airway clearance methods: Many methods are used for airway clearance. These procedures will not affect eligibility.

- Feeding tube: During sleep, a feeding tube may be needed to provide the body with the essential nutrients.

- Bowel surgery. Bowel surgery may be needed to remove the obstruction.

- Endoscope and flushing: Mucus is aspirated from blocked airways through an endoscope.

- Removal of the Nasal Polyps: May be required if it interferes with breathing.

The conclusion of this treatment is that;

They won't affect the underwriting process

What you should expect from the Insurance companies

Lower Rates with Instant Coverage – There Won't be a Waiting Period

The simplified or level insurance policy has the most affordable monthly premiums without a waiting period, meaning immediate coverage from day one and complete death benefits for the beneficiaries.

There are many world-class insurers that can provide a simplified treatment plan for cystic fibrosis, and we have happened to represent many of them.

Higher Monthly Premium

You will still get this from a top-rated insurer, and it is the next best option if you are not eligible for the level or simplified policy.

This is also a good plan, even though the rates are a little higher, the best part is that the coverage will be immediate from day one.

Immediate Percentage Payment or More After Awhile

This is often referred to as a Graded plan with higher monthly premiums and annual percentage payments.

- From 30 to 40% within the first 12 months

- From 70 to 80% within the second 12 months

If you are able to complete the waiting period of 24 months, the full benefit will be paid to your beneficiaries.

Higher Premium and Full Waiting Period Combined

This will be available to the highest risk candidates.

This is a kind of normal policy for many insurance companies for candidates considered to be at higher risk. It is quite simple; you will have a higher monthly payment and a waiting time of at least 24 months.

TIP: Compare the Guarantee Issue plan with the one mentioned above; you can also inquire with one of our professionals to determine the best option for you.

Guaranteed Issue (GI) Plan

As with what has already been said about lung transplants for cystic fibrosis, this is your last resort.

As simply stated, your acceptance is guaranteed inasmuch as you have the legal right to contract. There will be no questions or analysis of drug history.

You can have your GI plan approved by phone in 30 minutes.

Because of the greater risk that insurers are willing to accept, the monthly premiums will be much and there will be a compulsory 24 months waiting time. In addition, if it happens that you pass away in the waiting time, your beneficiaries will be eligible for the total of what you have paid with 10% interest.

Brutally Honest Guide to Burial Insurance with Arthritis

For seniors, or anyone for that matter, arthritis is no fun, and this is why we exist to make sure that you receive a *top-notch, low-cost* final expense insurance company to insure you. Thankfully, arthritis will not hinder the process of getting affordable insurance that fits your needs.

With decades of experience, we are confident that we can help you establish a plan for handling your final expense, even with arthritis. And it has never been easier.

We offer a simple phone interview process to remove any worry about writing, which may not be an easy task. In our phone interview, which is handled via the voice signature application, we ask a few questions regarding your situation to properly assess which insurance company will be the best fit for you. We have had countless clients refer their friends after their positive experience with us, so let us help you get the right policy you need!

Arthritis and Burial Insurance

Typically, it can be challenging to find burial insurance with a serious health condition. Conditions such as heart disease or cancer could cause an insurance company to decline final expense insurance benefits, but not arthritis.

Qualifying for immediate, full-coverage death benefits will be no problem with an arthritis diagnosis with any company. And since there are no requirements for medical exams or physicals, complete approval can be granted in a matter of minutes after the successful completion of a medical questionnaire.

Arthritis can restrict your ability to live within a regular, daily routine, but it will not limit your capability to secure burial insurance. Assuming arthritis is the only health condition you have, in obtaining it, it's as if the arthritis is nonexistent!

So, considering how burial insurance companies view an arthritis diagnosis, you can expect coverage at the lowest possible rate.

Arthritis and the Underwriting Process

Remember how we said earlier that arthritis would not cause a burial insurance company to deny your coverage? That is because no insurance company will include it on the health questionnaire in the underwriting process. So, if this is your only pre-existing condition, there will be no issues with securing your coverage.

It is just like you never had to deal with the underwriting at all!

What Are the Types of Arthritis that are Deemed Okay by the Insurance Companies?

- Rheumatoid arthritis

- Septic arthritis

- Gout

- Osteoarthritis

- Psoriatic arthritis

With any of these, any final expense insurance company will offer you coverage. At SuperMutual.com, not only do we work with the best insurance companies, we can help you find the most desirable final expense coverage with one of them.

Arthritis and Medications

Just like arthritis, medications will not hinder the process of underwriting burial insurance. None of the medicines used to treat arthritis will be an issue.

Common arthritis medications that cause no problem at all:

- Azathioprine

- Azasan

- Azulfidine

- Celebrex

- Hydroxychloroquine

- Imuran

- Methotrexate

- Plaquenil

- Rituxan

Assuming arthritis is your only pre-existing condition, this process will be a breeze.

Arthritis and Potential Complications

So here is where it is beneficial to speak with a final expense insurance specialist with our experience level. There are some scenarios in which a plan would be more complicated.

Wheelchairs

We understand that sometimes arthritis can be so debilitating that a wheelchair may be necessary. Though the need to use a wheelchair does reduce the number of insurance companies available to you, they do not entirely rule out the possibility of having burial insurance. Insurance plans from other companies will cost more and include a twenty-four-month wait. Since we represent many acclaimed burial insurance companies, wheelchair use due to arthritis is okay with them.

Activities of Daily Living (ADLs) and Denial of Coverage for Arthritis

Should you discover that you require a home healthcare assistant's help with day-to-day activities, your insurance options will be limited further. Insurance companies define ADLs as being any of the below activities:

- Dressing

- Bathing

- Using the restroom

- Taking medication

- Eating

If arthritis, or any other pre-existing condition, causes you to need assistance with any of the above-listed activities, immediately getting inexpensive final expense insurance coverage will be considerably more difficult. The only available insurance company that will cover you will be Royal Neighbors of America.

Royal Neighbors of America is the only company that is okay with someone accepting help with ADLs. If you do not qualify due to other pre-existing conditions, your last option will be to go to Gerber Life for a guaranteed issue life policy.

These plans have no medical questionnaires or checks, but they do come with a waiting period of twenty-four months. Gerber Life would refund your premiums plus 10 percent if you were to pass away during this time. Once the two years are complete, the policy would protect you like any other comparable: in full, for life.

Of course, the Gerber Life scenario is considered the final option and not for you if you are only dealing with arthritis.

Just because you have other conditions, you may still qualify for a simplified plan, but it may be a close call. Please call us to assist you and your situation better, as we are delighted to help you find the best insurance company.

Arthritis and Affordable Burial Insurance

As you have read up to this point, we have repeatedly mentioned that we will have no problem finding an insurance company for you. All you have to do now is call, and we can get you the most suitable deal for your situation.

With over 35 years of experience our team of final expense insurance specialists have the passion for insuring anyone with arthritis with the best available burial insurance policy and additional features at no extra cost.

THE SECRET TO GETTING BURIAL INSURANCE WITH HOME HEALTH CARE

One of the toughest aspects of getting older can be planning for the future of your loved ones after you're gone. It's a very frightening thought to consider that you'll no longer be here. In addition to that, your friends and family will hold a funeral after you have passed.

Most people plan their retirement by deciding how their remaining funds can last until the end of their lives. It is important to figure out the amount of money it'll take to cover the expenses needed for the funeral.

So if you are trying to figure that out, it means you're ahead of the game. Those that plan accordingly ahead can reduce the financial burden on their families by choosing an affordable burial insurance policy.

Deciding to buy funeral insurance, and which policy to go with is not an easy decision because, like most insurance policies, burial insurance has its own rules.

What exactly is Burial Insurance?

Simply stated, burial insurance is a policy made to cover death-related costs for someone, and there are various forms and names such as final expense insurance, funeral insurance, and pre-need insurance. Essentially, these policies are all the same thing, but there are some minor differences.

Burial insurance and final expense insurance

These policies are also called life policies or whole life policies. They are bought directly from an insurance company, and not from a funeral home.

Generally, they cost less than pre-need insurance and will have a beneficiary and not a burial service provider. Most people prefer this because it does not force you to use a particular funeral home, but you stand the risk of your named beneficiary not spending the funds as planned.

Pre-need funeral insurance

This is usually provided by a burial home or a burial service provider. Most times, it is a whole-life policy linked to an underlying insurance company. An important quality of this policy is that it sometimes has the burial service provider as the beneficiary. Once you pay, the provider takes care of the funeral when you die.

That may seem better, but it can cause issues if you relocate or die elsewhere and cannot use another funeral home. These policies are also more expensive than others. However, one benefit of this policy is that they mostly issue out payment as soon as the person dies, while regular life insurance policies sometimes take several days.

Is it a Must to Have Funeral Insurance?

It depends on various factors and preferences. At times, people will say that their beneficiaries should make use of their standard life insurance for their funeral expenses. But others want their loved ones to be able to get the entire amount of their regular life insurance, so they will buy a smaller kind of whole life insurance to serve as their funeral insurance.

When they do this, their family and loved ones will be able to use that policy to cover expenses such as:

- **Memorial services:** including refreshments and a venue where the service will hold.

- **Funeral services:** including the car services to use to the burial site.

- **Coffins and burial costs:** to pay for the cost of labor to dig the plot and maintenance, and the actual burial land.

- **Cremations:** they will have to cover the cost of cremation and an urn or box to pour the ashes in.

So, for most people, the final expense policy is a must. Leaving loved ones to cover the costs of the funeral and other expenses is just not an option, and they want to ensure there is enough money left to cover these needs.

How much is Burial Insurance?

Most funeral insurance plans are around $20,000 or less. But don't let that scare you, that is not the end of the world. These are whole life policies and due to this, do not expire.

In most instances, you can get the right policy for $10,000 for men and women. But you should consider the funeral expenses you want to be covered by the burial insurance policy and see if you need extra for offsetting debts.

Is it Possible to Get Affordable Funeral Insurance on Home Health Care?

Now that you know what burial insurance policy is, you need to look for ways to get an affordable policy. There are scenarios where insurance companies flag applications because the applicant is on home health care. Those companies are not the right ones for you. But how can you get this vital insurance coverage?

Home Health Care Underwriting

As you apply for a burial insurance plan, the insurance companies will ask you a lot of questions. Also, they will run a prescription history check to verify your health issues.

When it comes to your home health care, the only thing you need to consider is the health question. There is nothing on a prescription history that will show if you were on home health care.

What are the Home Health Care Questions?

All funeral insurance company asks applicants if they have home health care. With that, below you will find the three common ways insurance companies may ask about home health care.

- If you have received home health care in the last 12 months

- If you are presently receiving, or been advised to get home health care

- If you are now, or within the last year getting home health care as a result of a chronic sickness

You will notice that these questions ask about home health care uniquely. That's important to remember when you consider your circumstances for home health care. You need to know what to expect when you go to get funeral insurance.

How to Buy Burial Insurance

- ### Determine your burial expenses

You need to begin by knowing the amount needed to pay for your funeral. The cost of your burial is important and needs to be considered first. It is usually the highest single cost.

Other burial expenses to consider include the remaining medical bills, living expenses, legal costs, and credit card bills.

- **Estimate if you'll leave behind sufficient money to cover the final costs**

The important question to ask is if there will be enough money to cover your final expenses. You may need to speak to a financial advisor to determine this. The company should immediately give your survivors access to the money to pay your funeral bills.

Don't let your money get tied up in probate. That could be a problem because burial providers expect payment at the time of the burial. There will probably be other expenses that come due upon your demise.

- **Determine if you need burial insurance**

If you do not expect to have sufficient money at the end of your life to cover your burial expenses, then a burial insurance policy might be best for you. Even if you leave behind sufficient funds, you may not want your burial costs to deplete that amount. It is best to have a burial insurance policy to make sure that your entire assets will be available to your loved ones.

- **Decide the insurance policy to go with**

There are various policies available today to help people cover their final expenses. An insurance coverage typically costs $10,000 to $30,000. The lower coverage is because these insurance policies are made to pay only enough for your burial, and not to give additional income to your family.

Brutally Honest Guide to Burial Insurance with Chronic Back Pain

It's quite difficult getting a good life insurance these days at a decent price, its little wonder patients with chronic back pain appreciates the importance of a standard life insurance. Nevertheless, there are several factors that determine getting a life insurance for a severe back pain.

Although, we can offer you at Regular or Standard rate

Throughout this article you will be given a brief on how we aid our clients in getting the best life insurance rates.

Life Insurance with Back Pain

Pain can come in varying degrees of severity, whether it's a headache or a stomach pain, these kinds of pain can be dealt with, however, for a chronic back pain, it's quite different because on the extreme, it can be life threatening.

Chronic back pain has no gender and age restriction; hence it doesn't matter whether a person is young, or old, male or female, chronic back pain has no respect of persons. Looking for an affordable life insurance that deals with chronic back pain can be quite a difficult task:

If you inherited back issues such as Ankylosing Spondylitis or other issues with spine alignment, or if you have Scoliosis or Osteoporosis, you can understand how painful and life-restricting this pain can be.

Apparently, there may also be various causes of Chronic Back Pain, such as a car crash or accidents at work, which causes back and spine injuries.

Hence, any of this may cause severe damage to a person delicate nerve ending, in the spinal area and would probably result in the Chronic back pain patients can relate to well.

Life Insurance is essential for any person and even Chronic Back Pain sufferers ought to have access to adequately affordable insurance coverage that will accommodate all of their conditions and eventually cover their families if possible.

Life Insurance Rates Influenced by Chronic Back Pain

One of the major causes of depression is the chronic back pain and sometimes the drugs and medication that are often prescribed are somewhat addictive rather present a cure. Also, this could lead to complications when on the quest for a life insurance because it can add to the premium paid.

In some cases, some people could be overdosed as a result of severe pain, therefore the insurance company must be aware of all medications taken whether prescribed administered by a medical specialist or not.

Both of these considerations must be taken into account by the insurance underwriters when delivering a life insurance offer, as if they are not aware of all the details, they would not be able to offer an offer that accurately represents the individual's needs.

As a result of this, it is important that we only partner with independent life insurance firms that are professionals who know how to select the right providers for people currently struggling with back pain.

The Best Options for Chronic Back Pains are Independent Life Insurance Agencies

Obviously, you would want an all-encompassing life insurance, which takes into account all your needs, your chronic back pain and most importantly, very much affordable.

You must also understand that you have covered all possible scenarios and also provided for your loved ones, thus an all-encompassing life insurance is an essential requirement.

In order to get the best insurance coverage that is affordable, the right approach to do this is to consult an independent life insurance company, like ourselves.

An Independent life insurance provider understands and knows how to manage a high-risk life insurance industry and have a wide basket of life insurance firms to choose from. While using option to buy life insurance, you will basically browse for all providers at the same time before you are either eligible for coverage or find the competitive monthly rates that you seek.

For instance:

We are very experienced in dealing with all type of chronic back problems and you get the best value for your time and money with our service, because we offer services that are tailored to your individual needs, also is sure that you will be getting all the services at an affordable rate.

How is a Quote Being Prepared for Individuals with Back Pain by Life Insurance Companies?

In order to allow an independent life insurance provider to offer you the best quality of work quote personalized to your individual needs, they need to ask you some thorough questions, these questions are designed to find out about your unique Back Pain issues and causes, and also to find out what type of life insurance you need.

The information needed to precisely tailor a quote can differ; however, they include the following questions:

- What is the source of pain in the back?

- When did the back pain begin?

- Can the back pain stop or in some way limit your life?

- What medications or medicines are you taking at the moment?

- Has your doctor recommended these drugs / medications?

- The specifics of the pain: is there a constant pain? Is that sporadic pain? How long is the pain going to last?

- How long have you been suffering from back pain?

You should ensure that when you do provide answers to these questions, you must provide honest and sincere answers, as honest answers are vital to providing you with the best possible level of insurance coverage.

You don't have to lie about anything, because every information is so important, because the wrong information could adversely affect the service rendered to you.

Furthermore, it is important that you provide as much detail as possible because, in order for us to establish a clear perspective of your lifestyle and insurance needs. Keep in mind that it's only when all these information are provided that we can comprehensively understand the level of coverage that you will need.

If you make the mistake of not providing all the details and facts, also if you try to hide them in anyway, the provided quote might not be as accurate as it should be, and it might lead to nonpayment when you most need it.

Disorder causing chronic back pain is quite common and most insurance company always look out for your circumstances and then provide a standard "one size fits all" kind of insurance coverage, also they do not always cover personalized life insurance to individual requirement.

The challenge with this is that everyone individual has a different back issues and different life insurance needs and also the prices for these types of coverage will vary dramatically, with high insurance premiums not necessarily providing the most appropriate standard of coverage available.

Getting Cost Effective Life Insurance Coverage with Chronic Back Pain

Now based on your individual back challenge, you could charge a much higher fee for your coverage, although if it's just a little issue then you could get lower charges. Then if the condition is very serious, you will most likely receive high risk premium.

Applicants that pose a higher risk to the insurance provider will pay more for life insurance.

The insurance provider needs to know how much risk you have for the coverage you need. If you would like lower prices, you need to be less risky.

If you ever worked with a local agent, you should understand how the procedure goes. You have the liberty to call and answer questions, and also get a quote. Most often they would try to convince you to purchase the most expensive plan and an additional insurance coverage.

If you have any concerns or question regarding life insurance, then we are just a phone call away.

The Secret to Getting Burial Insurance with Schizophrenia

If you have ever been told by someone that Schizophrenia would disqualify you from getting burial insurance or that you must pay a high premium, that person was wrong! To be sincere that there are a lot of companies that are okay with candidates that have this condition. We can get the cheapest funeral insurance that costs you right away!

We have a record of many satisfied customers who suffer from this disorder. They didn't pay more for insurance than someone without Schizophrenia! Today we're going to show you how we help them.

This article will discuss how insurers respond to closing final expenses for applicants with Schizophrenia, what their options are, and, most essentially, how you can find the best funeral plan around.

Life Insurance for Those with Mental Illness

It is inevitable to have your application rejected if you admit Schizophrenia (or the insurance company knows) prolonged episodes of depression, anxiety, or especially when candidates admit to having suicidal or self-harming thoughts.

Many insurance companies operate with outdated knowledge of Schizophrenia or other mental conditions.

We know that you will not allow yourself or someone you love to neglect Schizophrenia and that you will take care of yourself according to your medication plan and have a healthy lifestyle. That is why you would have more favorable options for your final insurance.

Fortunately, nowadays and in the insurance era, there are excellent A + insurers that have a good understanding of Schizophrenia and other mental illnesses and are open to anyone with mental health problems.

These top insurers have insurance policies primarily for clients with mental illness and can provide the most affordable payment costs with instant insurance coverage.

Underwriting for Schizophrenia

Probably, you want to pay the lowest and be covered in the quickest time possible, right? Definitely. Everyone does. To do this, you must apply for a funeral insurance plan with underwriting. The underwriting will cover only a few health questions and check the prescription history.

Using this information, the insurer can verify that you deserve to be approved for the lowest rating and instant protection. Through our agency, many applicants have gotten Level death benefits.

The Health Questions

As I said earlier, some companies inquire about this condition. The fact is that these questions can come in various forms. Remember that every company has its differences. With that in mind, here are probably all the different ways you can see questions about Schizophrenia:

- Did you have any diagnosis or treatment for any psychosis in the last 24 months?

- Were you hospitalized because of anxiety, depression, or other mental health disorder in the past 24 months?

- Did you have any diagnosis or treatment for mood disorder or severe depression in the last 24 months?

- Did you any diagnosis or treatment for Schizophrenia in the last 24 months?

Also, note that different companies have different times for their look back. Twenty-four months is undoubtedly the commonest. In comparison, some companies may ask questions about these things by looking back on 3 to 5 years or your whole life.

Medications that are Flagged by Insurers.

Like all other health conditions that has to do with lifestyle, the best way to manage Schizophrenia is communicating effectively with your doctor and following the advised treatment plan.

For life insurers that are concerned with Schizophrenia, below are some of the medications on their watchlist.

- Brexpiprazole

- Asenapine

- Aripiprazole

- Chlorpromazine

- Cariprazine

- Fluphenazine

- Haloperidol

- Clozapine

- Iloperidone

- Olanzapine

- Lurasidone

- Perphenazine

- Paliperidone

- Risperidone

- Quetiapine

- Ziprasidone

Different Options Burial Insurance Might Offer You Based on Your Result.

This is probably not surprising, but it is essential to put things in context. Every life insurer has different underwriting rules, and they all react in different ways to various health conditions. Below is a comprehensive list of all the responses that burial insurance providers can give when they meet an applicant with Schizophrenia.

They Will Give you a Waiting Period of Two Years and Charge More Premium.

First, some companies may charge 30% more and others up to 60% more. Every insurance company varies. However, if there is a waiting period, it will take two years. This means that there will not be payment of any benefit on the policy if you die in the first 24 months. If this happened, they would reimburse you for all premiums with interest. The interest is always 10% for many companies.

There Will be a Partial Waiting Period and a Little Premium.

In this case, they will ask you to pay 15 to 40% more. Also, they will specify that your policy will pay some percentage of the death benefit in the first year and a higher percentage in the second year. It is usually 30-40% in the first 12 months and 70-80% in the second year.

The Insurers will do Nothing.

As mentioned earlier, when starting this article, some companies might be less interested in Schizophrenia. For these companies, you have an equal benefit from someone who has no health problems. Thankfully, these companies allow you to get immediate coverage and affordable rates.

Hospitalization for Schizophrenia

To make this simple, some insurance companies will reject or make you pay you a higher payment cost with a waiting period.

These insurance companies do not have end-of-life insurance plans made for someone who is in hospital for a mental illness, particularly Schizophrenia.

However, suppose you contact Top-notch Final Expense Insurance professionals such as the ones we have at our agency. In that case, you will be provided with options from the Top-rated insurance companies in the country. Additionally, these companies have insurance plans that are best suited for Schizophrenia or other mental condition.

Also, the policies that are provided by them will be at an affordable rate and zero waiting period.

Brutally Honest Guide to Burial Insurance with Bipolar Disorder

As you might have probably known, the way to reduce funeral insurance rates is qualifying for a policy with some underwriting. With that, you'll find that most funeral insurers rarely worry about being bipolar.

The Conclusion of Everything is That

If you are searching for funeral insurance with bipolar disorder, you find that hardly any company will be concerned about it. You will effortlessly qualify for the simplified or Level rates with almost all insurers. There won't be a waiting period, and the minimum payment is required. Basically, 99% of end-of-life expense companies do not care that you have this condition.

What is Bipolar Disorder and Why It Impacts Life Insurance?

According to definitions, bipolar disorder is known as a mental illness and a brain disorder that changes the mood, activity levels of the patient, and the ability to perform daily activities.

It is a well-known disease, and according to the National Institute of Mental Health, this condition affects about 5.7 million adult Americans. According to the World Health Organization, it affects approximately 45 million around the world.

Until recently, initially, bipolar disorder was seen as a much severe medical problem than previously thought. It is now possible for someone who is bipolar to get full or temporary coverage at a very low price.

Even though there is also a risk for insurers, nowadays, they have more understanding of what that risk really is, compared to what they thought it would be a long time ago.

In fact, while working with clients that have bipolar disorders, we can be sure that they will receive a favorable offer as long as they do not have other serious medical problems.

However, this is good news.

Did you know that funeral insurance plans do not require you to undergo any physical examination or checking through medical records? Regardless of how this might sound, it is the truth. You only get to answer health questions.

Life can be challenging in many ways if you are bipolar. Luckily, there is a lot of effective treatment option that will enable you to live happily. Fortunately, you will find that your funeral insurance will no longer be expensive because it is bipolar, nor will it require you to go through a waiting period of any kind.

Underwriting Process for Bipolar Disorder

In short, the lowest rates are called simplified, Best, or level and they come with instant insurance coverage starting from day one depending on the insurer.

With this in mind, to become eligible for a simplified or level insurance plan, you must apply for funeral insurance or end-of-life expenses with simplified underwriting.

Also, for other health conditions for underwriting, there will be two aspects that insurers will consider for evaluation.

Underwriting Health Questions

For more emphasis, insurers pay little attention to mental health problems like bipolar disorder. The questions asked by insurance companies do not mention words such as bipolar, mania, depression and mania, etc.

That is, when an insurer does not particularly ask about a health illness, it means they are not really concerned about it and that it will have no issue with giving out final cost insurance with instant insurance coverage.

So, if your insurance agent says you may have a hard time finding a good insurer for bipolar disorder, it's time to move forward and change the agent.

At the same time, an insurer that will directly question you regarding bipolar disorder is scarce or does not even exist. Health problems may raise questions about other health conditions you may have.

Prescription History Evaluation

In addition, your health and prescription history will be checked if you have other health issues, the date, whether you undergo treatment, or for how long.

Another important thing to note is that being bipolar can result in having mental disorders like schizophrenia, depression/anxiety, and PTSD.

Bipolar Medications

Together with health questions, insurers will analyze your prescription history. Basically, this is to ensure your health is as you claimed it to be.

Many of the bipolar patients take many medications to control the condition. They are mood stabilizers, antipsychotics, antidepressants, anti-anxiety, and antidepressants-antipsychotics drugs.

Below is a list of bipolar prescription that funeral insurers will not have issues with. If you are taking any of these medications, you will not have any problem with the funeral insurers.

The only way to have problems with these prescriptions is if you apply to a company that is not fine with bipolar disorder. However, ensure you avoid this because there are many operators that accept this condition well.

- Aripiprazole
- Carbamazepine
- Effexor
- Lithium
- Asenapine
- Emasam
- Divalproex Sodium
- Lexapro
- Marplan
- Lamotrigine
- Nardil
- Olanzapine
- Lurasidone
- Paxil
- Parnate
- Quetiapine
- Prozac
- Remeron
- Valproic Acid
- Ziprasidone

- Risperidone
- Zoloft
- Wellbutrin

Types of Bipolar Disorder

According to the Manual on Diagnostic and Statistical Mental Disorders, below are the types of bipolar disorder.

Bipolar disorder 1: It involves one or more manic episodes of heavy mood swings from mania to depression. This can trigger psychotic episodes that can result in injuries and hospitalizations.

Bipolar Disorder 2: This is a softer type of mood swings, in which there is at least one depression or hypomania that alternates between episodes of severe depression that will last four days or more.

Cyclothymic disorder: Short episodes of hypomania alternate with short periods of short-term depressive symptoms, as seen in complete hypomanic episodes or episodes of total depression.

Mixed characteristics - At this stage, there is an occurrence of concurring symptoms of mood-altering polarities during manic, depressive, or hypomanic episodes. Commonly, the symptoms are high energy, insomnia, racing thoughts, and, at the same time, irritability, despair, hope, and suicide.

As stated earlier, it does not matter the type of bipolar you have; we have top-rated companies that can get you covered. For example, basically, you will be offered a Simplified or Level rates with instant insurance, hoping you do not have any serious health issues that can disqualify you.

Hospitalization

It is completely possible for someone with bipolar disorder to experience an episode that can cause temporary hospitalization. If you were hospitalized as a result of an episode, it would have little effect on your eligibility for funeral insurance.

The fact is that only a few selected insurers give you a health question asking if you have been in the hospital (for whatever reason) in the past 6 or 12 months. Because there are so many other insurers that are not concerned with this question, then hospitalization would not be an issue.

It is now clear that being bipolar is not a problem. At the same time, the way to get the best funeral insurance is really the same, irrespective of your health.

To get the best funeral insurance for bipolar disorder, you need to work with an independent broker who has access to several insurers.

Want to Find Out Something Really Interesting?

You don't even have to look for a broker like that.

As an independent agency, we have access to a number of insurers. We will check through the market and get you a final expense company that will offer you the best plan at an affordable price.

We do not have a special affiliation with any insurance company. Therefore, we can and will connect impartially with any carrier that best suits your needs.

How to Get the Best Burial Insurance Company with Bipolar Disorder.

In addition to the serious illnesses you may have, the only problem you may encounter if you have bipolar disorder when you apply for your final expense plan is that you are offered expensive policies with waiting periods. Furthermore, it means that you have hired the wrong insurance broker.

We can assist you in getting the best funeral insurance plan possible for bipolar disorder. Our team of specialists consists of experienced and accomplished insurance professionals who are passionate about finding the best funeral policy for applicants who have Bipolar disorder or other mental issues.

SURE-FIRE WAY TO GET BURIAL INSURANCE WITH DEPRESSION

Most life insurers are perfectly okay with people that have depression. In fact, it is rare to find a company that asks questions about depression when inquiring about your health. If you are depressed, you will be easily eligible to receive level death benefits in almost all end-of-life expense companies. This means your payment will be the lowest rate offered by insurers and be fully insured from the first day.

But it Gets Even Better ...

Since burial insurance policies are simplified, you will not have to present your medical records or undergo any form of examination. All you have to do is answer a few health questions. We can get official approval from the insurer in a few minutes!

Depression is a serious problem that affects a lot of Americans. This can hamper the daily routine of life. At the same time, what it will not do is impacting your funeral plan. So many companies accept this condition as they see it as if you don't have it.

The Underwriting Process of Burial Insurance Companies for Depression

Have you been denied life insurance because of depression...? The underwriting process is all about answering some questions about your health and checking your prescription history.

In some unusual cases, the combination of health conditions and medication might result in graded or decline. Be sincere with your agent; In most situations, we can get the coverage that will be effective from the first day because we have access to multiple insurers in a call.

 At any rate, you will be asked other questions if you may have other diseases in the past and present that they will have issues with.

In short, end-of-life insurance companies will evaluate all aspects of your health so that they know what type of insurance they can offer to match your risk level.

In the process of underwriting you, insurance companies will ask about this information:

- Questions about current and past illnesses (if any) and lifestyle.
- Evaluation of the history of prescription drugs

The Health Questions

Honestly, you can't really see a health questionnaire that will inquire about depression or antidepressants.

About 99% of funeral home providers do not ask about depression at all. If you see a mention of depression, they usually use the words major depression. The point is, if you need to get life insurance, depression is not a problem!

Medications

In addition to health questions, all funeral policies with underwriting will include a prescription history review. They do this as a way to check the status of your health. For instance, if someone who was treated for cancer this year answered no to the cancer question, it would be wrong to check the history of the prescription.

Finally, all types of drugs are flagged by many funeral insurers for different conditions. Some prescriptions may cause the insurers to see an applicant as being high risk. This can result in higher rates and wait times, depending on the insurer and the medication.

That said, this is a very comprehensive list of antidepressants. If you take any of them, we have companies that are perfectly okay with all of them. You might be taking one or more of these prescriptions, but you can still easily qualify for a minimal fee and immediate protection form many insurers.

- Abilify
- Amoxapine
- Amitriptyline
- Bupropion
- Citalopram
- Clomipramine
- Desvenlafaxine
- Doxepin
- Duloxetine
- Fluvoxamine
- Desipramine
- Escitalopram
- Fluoxetine
- Mirtazapine
- Isocarboxazid
- Nortriptyline
- Imipramine
- Levomilnacipran
- Phenelzine

- Nefazodone
- Selegiline
- Olanzapine
- Paroxetine
- Protriptyline
- Trimipramine
- Sertraline
- Seroquel
- Trazodone
- Venlafaxine
- Vortioxetine
- Vilazodone
- Tranylcypromine

Getting Life Insurance at Low Rates with Depression is Possible.

The best thing you can do is to be sincere with yourself about your health condition before you begin the process of underwriting, so there won't be surprises later.

If you have mild depression, inasmuch as you go to the right life insurer, you can still get preferred rates, as long as you meet all other preferential rate criteria. In unusual cases, some people have even obtained a preferred rate.

If you suffer from moderate depression, you are likely to be eligible for standard life insurance rates.

If you think you stand between mild and moderate, you can qualify for the standard plus.

For serious depression, your case will be examined individually. The underwriters will want to check your medical history, medication, and treatment records.

If you are still concerned about whether you will get approval or not or are nervous about what underwriters have to say, feel free to contact us to ask about the guaranteed acceptance life insurance policy.

We have dealt with a lot of people who have already suffered from depression, and we can help you get the most affordable rates possible, irrespective of your health condition.

WE GOT YOU COVERED: BURIAL INSURANCE FOR PEOPLE WITH COPD

Insurance companies survive and prosper by assessing accurately through the strictest of interviews and mathematical calculation the risk of any policy, regardless of its content. It goes without saying that quality burial insurance for those suffering from COPD, a disease that is the 4th leading cause of death in the United States, carries an especially high risk and very hard to find. Almost all insurance companies will directly ask about COPD or chronic lung disease, and much depends on your understanding of the process. The quality and cost of the insurance are all subject to negotiations usually, but not for COPD sufferers, and especially not those on oxygen therapy. Rejection is common.

You worry rightly concerning insurance that will cover the cost of funeral and burial is critical to ensure that your family will have the money they need when you pass away. While obtaining life insurance isn't easy with COPD, we have both good and bad news—and a great belief that with proper management, the best burial insurance for those diagnosed with COPD can be available. There are a few types of burial insurance for people with COPD. We will help you make sense of them. Not to worry. We can and will find you an affordable burial insurance plan, but you must be realistic. The news is good and bad.

The Bad News

There is no cure for COPD, though there are stages that are clearly marked and well-known to insurance agent calibrating and quantifying a disease which may heavily impact the quality of insurance policies that they will be offered, indeed whether one is offered at all. Much depends upon an accurate assessment of the stages and the specific form of COPD that sometimes comes from industrial solvents, but most often from smoking. Those who are under oxygen therapy or show similar signs of suffering at an advanced stage of the disease will have an agent directly reject your application.

The Good News

You can find with our help a top-rated A+ insurance company ready to offer someone who has COPD the kind of dream insurance that were not thought possible, starting on Day1, for the lowest cost and without a waiting time period. We offer a unique plan after considering the context and alternatives.

This is an extremely rare and precious find on our part. We found what may be the only reputable company fully ready to handle the risk of COPD applicants without costing more or incorporating any type of waiting period. It is something we will return after we review very limited alternatives and the reason why they are so rare for COPD sufferers.

How do Burial Insurance Companies Judge your Eligibility if you have COPD?

There is no easy answer to this question, though all variations have in common simply asking if you have it, sometimes without much follow up questions. Your history of prescription drugs will tell all that needs to be known from routine insurance on drug use. Actually, COPD cases are mostly caused by tobacco consumption over long time periods, but this information, as other life-style-related variables, is generally not readily accessible in routine claims, Whether or not you have COPD may be a sole consideration, and that is determined by the drugs you have been prescribed, how long have you taken these drugs and whether you use oxygen for breathing disorder, not sleep apnea.

The Stages of COPD

Stage 1 is hardly noticeable. You may suffer some shortness of breath, cough up some colored phlegm or show other symptoms long-time smokers rarely notice or even worry about at this stage. With the help of spirometry as a device, a simple breathing test will both identify the presence and the progress of the disease. You breathe in deeply and blow into a tube without, then with medication that opens up the airways.

Three numbers come together (a) how much air you exhale which is called forced vital capacity (FVC), (b) how much of that came out in the first second named forced expiratory capacity (FEV1) (c) from these numbers collectively is derived ling capacity. If your reading reaches 70 % or above, you are diagnosed with COPD, while FEV1 tells you the stage with higher than 80% establishing you in Stage 1. Stage 2 considerate moderate COPD, most likely without severe symptoms and most likely still ignored has FEV1 at 50-79%, Even at stage 3, most still ignore the intermittent but persistent symptoms becoming chronic with FEV1 assessed at 30-49%.

Unfortunately, by the time you know and had the most sever of symptoms and you answer positively to the question of whether you have COPD with FEV1 less than 30%, you have reached an irreversible end-stage. You have shortness of breath, made increased visits to the emergency department and become hospitalized with a condition that could easily veer into serious ling infection and respiratory failure. You have an inhaler and most substantial mechanical breathing aid to get by.

Clearly you are very high risk, for it is very likely that you had finally become aware that you have arrived at the terminal stage of the life cycle. There is now no special need to ask about your environment, lifestyle, or whether you had quit smoking when you can barely breath or get about without help. In fact, there is only a need to look into your medications to confirm your condition, which you know is bad news already.

Standard Medications for COPD

There are numerous drugs belonging to COPD treatment. Your insurance agent knows them all and will use online means to analyze the history of your varied medications to verify just that one crucial question, whether you have COPD, the sole category of risk analysis. We are talking your entire life history of prescription drug use because the disease may strike early, your drugs signifying COPD`s steady and inevitable advance. Practice varies by company, but if the long list of drugs in the following category is employed, late-stage COPD is inevitably suspected entirely based of certain medication combinations. Put differently, if you have been prescribed the following drugs and treatment modality, you will meet considerable obstacles getting insurance.

Short-acting bronchodilators cause airways to stay open to ease troubled breathing using an inhaler or nebulizer.

Long-acting bronchodilators are medications that are designed to treat COPD over a extended period of time.

Corticosteroids reduce inflammation that swell and irritate airways, making air flow easier in the lungs.

Methylxanthines has severe side-effects and employed only for the most severe cases. as an anti-inflammatory drug to relax the muscles in the airways, the significant cause of nausea or vomiting, tremors, headache, and trouble sleeping.

Combination drugs combine either two long-acting bronchodilators or an inhaled corticosteroid and a long-acting bronchodilator.

Triple therapy, a combination of an inhaled corticosteroid and two long-acting bronchodilators, may be used for severe COPD and flare-ups.

We Are on Your Side

This is our business, and we want to lower expectations to realistic and achievable levels. What is the bottom line? You need us to make a thorough assessment of your prescription drug use that will guide us to the appropriate kind of recommended coverage among competing firms offering burial insurance coverage. We will let you know with honesty and sensitivity but remind you that emphysema is considered a major disease with very high risk of mortality. We know with considerable certainty your level of risk and insurance options to advise you properly, even when our duty is to tell you that your application at your stage of the disease can.

We can see your need, but also know full well the statistics showing a decreased life expectancy of considerable magnitude, putting the insurance company that issues such a policy at risk. It would be worthwhile to look at matters from the point-of-view of the insurer. At the end of the day, statistics show that the five-year life expectancy rate for an individual who has been diagnosed with COPD can range from 40 to 70%.

What to Expect from Insurance Companies?

You may be thinking of applying for the kind of no medical exam term life insurance policy, though with pre-existing medical condition, such policies are out of reach to those diagnosed with pre-existing medical condition, especially one as severe as COPD in its final stages.

You may expect the following:

Higher Premium

The rate may vary from 15% to 40% additional premium payment to offset the attendant risks of the policy. There are huge benefits in receiving 100% of the policy from Day 1. Such insurance companies are by no means plentiful. We need to keep a vigilant eye on the market to find firms ready to offer such policies to our clients.

Extended Waiting Period

Given that you are most likely in a very advanced state of the disease, that your policy only comes into play after 24 months is no small matter, but it may be the only option. To be sure, if you pass away during the waiting period, the insurance company returns your deposit plus 10%.

Graded Plan

Such plan means that your beneficiaries receive fully 100% of the insurance payments, but not all at once. Indeed, there may be only 30% of the payment issued in the first year, with the rest distributed over the following year.

Penalties

These vary for final expense companies and include onerous waiting periods, higher fees and still other conditions, though for more money, some benefits will be paid promptly.

They will do nothing.

They will run a check on your medications and refuse you with varying explanations. This, sadly, is the most likely scenario.

Our Recommendation: The Guaranteed Issue Plan

The bottom line: if you are on oxygen therapy, you may no option whatever, and most certainly not the guaranteed issue burial insurance policy which has no medical exam. The fact is that such a plan is not only your best option, but indeed the only possible one.

It seems beyond your reach, yet we had found what has been until now the only insurance underwriter with credibility ready to issue such a plan,

This plan is astonishingly straightforward and appealing in its coverage terms. You are guaranteed to be accepted without any medical check-up or even a health questionnaire to trouble you. Give them your name, beneficiary and fulfill payment obligations, and you are in with some reservations in this instance.

There is a two-year waiting period and a higher premium, but consider carefully, you are on oxygen, and such plans are found nowhere else—though we keep searching.

You may be on oxygen and lacking a plan to pay for your funeral expenses. Time is of the essence to reduce the waiting period. Let's be frank. Your use of oxygen alone tells of the severity of your condition You would face certain denial elsewhere, Get in touch with us. We will steer you to a plan that will ease the grief and the debt-burden on your family.

Much depends on it.

THE MOST AFFORDABLE BURIAL INSURANCE FOR PATIENTS WITH CHRONIC BRONCHITIS

The fourth leading cause of death in the United States is chronic obstructive pulmonary disease (COPD) and most insurers consider it a high risk. Most funeral insurance companies charge higher premiums from time to time and may impose penalties.

Although some companies do not see chronic bronchitis as highly risky, meaning you won't be charged higher premiums or even make you endure a waiting period. We have a long history of helping people with chronic bronchitis get the ultimate cost insurance at the lowest cost. Today, we will provide you with a complete overview of the processes involved in buying burial insurance with chronic bronchitis condition.

This article will show you how insurers respond to people with chronic bronchitis, what options you have, and how you can get the best plan. Because this is a chronic and incurable disease, most companies do not respond well.

However, there are some insurance companies that offer a level of a benefit plan for death despite chronic bronchitis. Two things are involved here. First of all, your payment will be the same as someone who is in excellent health condition. Secondly, there will be complete coverage to protect you immediately. Remember, there aren't many companies that provide this incredible value, so we hope you don't have other health issues that can prevent you from qualifying. You will find companies that offer plans that will release some of your benefits in the first two years or none outside of these companies. In addition to the limited benefit or no benefit in the first two years, you will also receive higher premium levels.

The Best Life Insurance for Older People with COPD

There are some prestigious insurers who can offer the best quality funeral or final expense insurance for seniors at the lowest cost. For example, this is commonly referred to as a simplified, preferred, or level plan. However, we will be using simplified.

Simplified insurance has the lowest monthly premiums without a waiting period, which means immediate coverage from the first day, with a complete death benefit.

Therefore, we hope that you will only have chronic bronchitis as a serious medical condition and that you will not have any other illnesses or health problems that would prevent you from obtaining simplified insurance policy from these leading insurers.

Can I Get Life Insurance for COPD?

Similar to all funeral insurers, the insurance company will try to learn all everything about your disease's history, lifestyles, and living conditions by asking questions about illness and health issues, also your prescription history.

Almost all insurers will ask you a direct question about COPD, or they will usually ask if you have chronic lung disease, and you need to answer it in the affirmative.

Bad news

Because there is no cure for chronic bronchitis, and it can lead to various types of chronic lung disease, many funeral insurers have strict rules and regulations for assessing applicants with COPD.

From the moment chronic bronchitis is identified, other life insurance carriers will check the frequency and severity of your bronchitis. Depending on the insurance company, there will be various penalties to offset the rate of your risk.

Other insurers might not have an insurance policy to cover the risk of chronic bronchitis; therefore, they simply reject your application. There are many final expense insurers that don't want to have anything to do about chronic bronchitis or COPD of any kind. And that's why you need to contact an insurance agent who is very experienced.

Good news

As you have already known, chronic bronchitis cannot be cured, but the key to improving the patient's condition is to prevent their provoking factors.

In these days of medicine and insurance, there are many new and effective ways to prevent or control the symptoms of chronic bronchitis, and the country's leading insurance companies are aware of this. Even if you have severe chronic bronchitis or other serious medical conditions, we will always get the best and cheapest insurance plan.

These insurance plans will continue to come from the premium insurance companies that are accessible to us. Another good news is that you won't be needing medical or physical exams for the burial insurance plan.

So how do you get a simplified insurance policy? You will be required to undergo the underwriting process.

The Underwriting Process for Chronic Bronchitis

All funeral insurers will take you through a process before you can be qualified. Mostly, they will ask you many formal health questions. Also, they will assess your prescription history. Both will provide all the data necessary to inform you whether you will be approved or not.

Health Questions about Chronic Bronchitis

Most life insurance companies will ask you if you have chronic bronchitis. Keep in mind that some do not use the word "chronic bronchitis" specifically. They may use phrases such as chronic lung disease.

You will also notice that most funeral insurance companies will ask if you have had this condition at some point in your life. They do this because it is a chronic condition that cannot be cured. However, there are companies that associate a certain period (for example, in the last two years) to questions about chronic bronchitis.

Finally, most companies combine chronic bronchitis, emphysema, and COPD into a question.

Below are some examples of how funeral insurance companies can ask questions about it.

- Have you been or have you ever been treated for chronic bronchitis, emphysema, or COPD?

- In the past 24 months, have you received or been prescribed treatment for emphysema, chronic bronchitis, or COPD?

- Have you ever sought treatment or are currently being treated for COPD, emphysema, or any chronic lung disease other than asthma?

If you have chronic bronchitis, you should answer any of these questions in the affirmative.

Note

Some burial insurance companies will ask you about the stage of COPD you are, and this can have a big impact on the quality of the insurance plans you will get

In addition, some insurers will reject your application if you are in the severe stage of chronic bronchitis, COPD.

There are several funeral insurance companies that do not ask about chronic bronchitis or chronic lung disease. Since they are not asking about it, it means they have no problem with people that has this condition. You will find the best price and coverage for these companies.

Chronic Bronchitis Treatments

Most patients with this condition will receive various bronchodilators or drug prescriptions. There are many different bronchodilators sold, some of which are also used to treat emphysema or COPD.

Some of the drugs are;

- Analgesics/antipyretics

- Antimicrobials

- Antitussives/expectorants

- Antiviral Agents

- Bronchodilators

- Inhaled Corticosteroids

- Systemic Corticosteroids

Some of the popular bronchodilators are;

- Albuterol - Short acting bronchodilators

- Arcapta(Indacaterol)Ultra-long-acting-Beta Adrenoreceptor Agonist

It is a Bronchodilator

- Anoro - It is LABA bronchodilator

- Atrovent:- (ipratropium), a common bronchodilator

- Brovana - It is LABA bronchodilator

- Combivent - Bronchodilator

- Incruse - Bronchodilator

- ProAir - Use as bronchodilator in all ages

- Perforomist- (formoterol), a Bronchodilator cures COPD

- Stiverdi (Olodeterol) , a LONG-ACTING bronchodilator

- Spiriva (Tiotropium) , a common bronchodilator

- Seebri - a common bronchodilator, Used for COPD

- Stiolto - A combination of olodaterol and tiotropium. A common bronchodilator

- Tudorza -(Aclidinium), a common bronchodilator, used to cure bronchospasms

- Utibron - It contains (Indacaterol), an Ultra-long-acting-Beta-Adrenoreceptor Agonist

- Xopenex - A common bronchodilator

Important Things to Know

We cannot give you a clear formula to follow concerning the prescriptions. In fact, the underwriting process is different for every funeral life insurance company. For example, some companies classify people taking Brovana as a COPD patient.

On the other hand, another company may not consider Brovana's prescription as a sign that someone has a COPD condition.

After all, you will need a highly qualified agency like ours to go through your medications and see which companies would accept you with your health and medications.

However,

The application process also includes your prescription history. If you are under medication for chronic bronchitis, you cannot hide it. Even if you answered 'no' to their health question about chronic bronchitis (although a terrible idea), your drug history would negate your denial.

Can I Still Get Coverage with Oxygen Therapy?

Suppose your doctor has prescribed oxygen therapy for you, especially with a Venturi mask. In that case, it could mean that your chronic bronchitis is becoming severe, that you are prone to hypoxemia or low blood oxygen levels.

In a case like this, the only insurance option you can get is the Guaranteed Issue plan. If you have concluded securing a final expense insurance plan, we recommend that you sign up for that plan immediately.

Most insurers reject applications from COPD patient that are prescribed for oxygen therapy. It simply means that they do not have a guaranteed issue policy for anyone with chronic lung disease.

How would you feel after going through the underwriting process, and then you are later rejected? It will be a waste of time for you, thinking about the time you spent applying; it could be more frustrating.

By working with one of our final expense insurance specialists you can make this process painless. What our insurance experts will only need from you is a little bit of your time for your details.

Burial Insurance Companies and Different Insurance Plans for Chronic Bronchitis

After undergoing the underwriting process with health issues and evaluating your medication history, insurers to cover the final funeral costs will get back to you with insurance offers that match your level of risk following their rules and guidelines.

Always remember that each insurer will have its own standards for assessing your general health and will have different qualifications for an insurance policy.

Now, every aspect of your health becomes a vital factor in the types of insurance policies that will be issued to you.

At this stage, when you have honestly answered all the questions about the application, it is very important to check your expectations.

Lowest Rates with No Waiting Time

If you have been following this article from the beginning, you will remember that we mentioned a possibility like this.

This is a simple insurance plan. It will have the lowest rate for the monthly premiums without a waiting period, meaning there will be immediate coverage from day one, with a full death benefit for your beneficiaries.

The description of the simplified coverage is quite simple; however, it is important to understand that their conditions that qualify you for the simplified insurance plan as it is often offered to people that are completely healthy.

This is definitely what you need, and our client's satisfaction and happiness give us pleasure; we will work together with you to get an amazing plan like this for chronic bronchitis.

Only a few highly rated insurance companies can offer a simplified insurance plan for chronic bronchitis COPD. They all have different questions and conditions before you can qualify for their plan.

Therefore, we urge you to call us to ask questions about your eligibility for the simplified plan from these top-level insurers.

All we need is the details of your health and medication so that we can assess which of the few insurers will provide the lowest rate with your health condition.

Insurance Plan with a Higher Monthly Premium

This is also from a top-rated insurer and will be another best option if you do not qualify for the simplified policy option.

This insurance plan is 15 – 40% costlier than the simplified insurance plan. Similar to the simplified insurance plan, there is immediate coverage for this policy, that is, the death benefit will be fully paid to the beneficiary if you pass away beginning from the first day of your plan.

Because of the chronic bronchitis COPD nature, this is also an excellent plan; although the rates are slightly higher, the best part is that coverage will be instantaneous from day one.

Again, only a few insurance companies can offer this plan (same as the simplified), and we also represent them.

A Policy with 24 months Waiting Period With a 10% Interest

This will be applicable for candidates with high-risk chronic bronchitis, and it will have a waiting period to serve as compensation for the risk. Generally, the waiting period is at least 24 months, however, if pass away at any time during the waiting period, all of your payments will be reimbursed with a 10% interest rate payable to beneficiaries.

The advantage of this option is that your beneficiaries will also receive more money than your payment at the appropriate time.

In addition, another reason you should leverage on this option is that it is better than Certificates of deposit (CD) or Share Certificate in banks. No bank CD or share certificate will return 10% of your interest.

Graded Plan – Receive a Percentage of Benefits for the First 2 Years

This also applies to a high-risk candidate.

If an insurer offers you an option like this, it is best to consult an experienced burial insurance specialist to know if this option is right for you.

If you pass away in the first 12 months, a percentage of your total death benefit will be paid and a higher percentage for 13-24 months.

This is commonly referred to as a Graded plan, and here is the percentage of the payout.

- The first 12 months – 30%

- On the 13 to 24 months – 70%

After completing the 24 months waiting period, your beneficiaries will receive the full amount (100%)

Combination of Higher Rates and Waiting Times

This is offered for applicants with higher risk.

This policy is common for many insurers, for candidates who they consider having the highest risk. It is quite simple, a monthly premium at a higher cost of 15 to 40% with a waiting period of at least 24 months - and depending on the insurer, there may or may not be a benefit (within the waiting period). Thus, other companies may have a payment plan, like the graded plan (percent per year).

Tip: Sometimes, a guaranteed issue plan from a top-rated insurer is much more profitable or reasonable than the fourth and fifth option to check, do your calculations or consult with us.

In the end, you will be the one to decide; you can enquire one of our burial insurance specialists to know if this is the right option for you.

And always keep it in mind that above all, you come first, even before the insurance companies.

Guaranteed Issue (GI) Plan

As the name implies, you are guaranteed acceptance as long as you are legally competent to enter a contract or have a legal guardian. You will not answer questions as regards your health or have them review the history of your medication.

We can certainly have your GI plan approved in 10 minutes over the phone.

Because of the highest risk that insurers are willing to take, there will be higher monthly premiums, and they will have a strict waiting period of 24 months. In addition, if you pass away at any time during the waiting period, all your payments will be returned to the beneficiaries at a rate of 10%.

This insurance plan is solely for people who are seriously ill and have decided to be prepared when the day comes, to provide their family peace of mind - making sure that this option is always a good decision.

The Secret to Getting Burial Insurance with Sleep Apnea

When patients of sleep apnea start thinking about insurance policies, they typically wonder if their CPAP supplies are covered by insurance, or if their sleep study will be covered by insurance. Of course, these are vital concerns, but with the proper insurance policy, the plans will cover sleep apnea testing and supplies. And that is good.

What is Sleep Apnea?

Sleep apnea can be defined as periodic pauses in breathing while sleeping. These pauses can either be complete or incomplete apneas. Most people struggle with this and it can be scary. It can be potentially dangerous by causing serious complications like heart disease or other metabolic diseases.

This condition causes disruptions in breathing while sleeping. Typically, a person suffering from sleep apnea will stop breathing during sleep for some time. The person will then begin breathing again, at times, with a snorting sound.

These disruptions often transform someone from a state of deep sleep to a state of a lighter sleep, which causes daytime drowsiness. People suffering from the condition mostly don't know until someone notifies them of the problem.

Types of Sleep Apnea

Some types of sleep apnea to watch out for include:

- **Obstructive sleep apnea**

This is the most common kind of sleep apnea. It occurs when the throat muscles relax, causing the air passage to squeeze due to an obstruction, like big tongue, swollen tonsils, or the closing of the soft tissue of the throat when the muscles relax. Obstructive sleep apnea can be caused by obesity or anatomical proportions in the jaw.

- **Central sleep apnea**

It happens when the brain doesn't send the right signals to the muscles that control your breathing. A contributing factor to this condition is heart disease.

- **Complex sleep apnea**

It is also referred to as treatment-emergent central sleep apnea. It happens if a person has both obstructive and central sleep apnea.

Risk Factors

Sleep apnea may occur in young and old, male and female. Even kids can have this condition. But some factors put you at increased risk such as:

- Obesity
- Large neck circumference
- Narrow airway
- Males, especially those over age 65
- Family history
- Tranquilizers, sedatives, or alcohol
- Smoking
- Hypertension
- Sitting for a long time
- Heart disease

- Brain disorders
- Stroke

Treatment and Prevention

CPAP: Most people with sleep apnea are successfully treated by using a CPAP (Continuous Positive Airway Pressure) machine.

BIPAP: Unlike a CPAP, a BiPAP machine has two pressure settings: one for inhalation, and a lower pressure for exhalation which provides more comfort for the patient. (Bilevel Positive Airway Pressure)

Surgery: Some patients undergo surgery to get rid of excess tissue from the soft palate to try to relieve symptoms.

Changing sleeping position: Sleeping on the side of the body and not on the back can help some patients.

Consequences of Untreated Sleep Apnea

Sleep apnea can have severe consequences if you fail to treat it. This disorder causes several other conditions such as high blood pressure, diabetes, stroke, and heart disease. It can lead to memory issues, headaches, depression, impotence, and increase in weight. It has even been linked to car accidents caused by patients sleeping while driving.

What Life Insurance Companies Want

These companies are concerned that people with sleep apnea are doing the right things to keep it under control. A life insurance company will be looking at:

- Data to prove the prescribed treatment works for the patient.
- Regular use of the CPAP machine.

- Response to treatment.
- Constant follow-ups with the doctor.
- Diagnosis of risk factors, like heart disease, depression, hypertension, stroke, or obesity.
- Avoiding sleep-related accidents while driving.

The rating class given by insurance companies on applicants with this condition will depend on how chronic the illness is, results of previous studies, symptoms, treatment, response rates, compliance with treatment prescribed, when last symptoms occurred, and your overall health.

If left untreated, this condition is mostly rated poorly or may not be even be rejected for coverage, as are people who have the disorder but are not complying with the treatment recommendations. The insurance company will look at medical records to ensure that treatment is followed and is successful.

Preparing for Life Insurance Application

- Follow the treatment recommended by your doctor.
- Complete a post-treatment sleep study to prove that you're responding well to the treatment.
- Regularly attend follow-up visits to your doctor.

Can you be Denied Insurance?

Having this disorder should not be a reason for your insurance to be denied. But if other known risk factors are present, it could lead reduce your chances of getting insurance.

Also, the level of treatment you are under can influence the decision of an insurance company to consider your application. The company can rate you unfavorably if you fail to give evidence that you are presently receiving a form of treatment for your condition.

It is true that in most cases, funeral insurance companies can be friendlier and flexible to give insurance to those individuals who have some risk factors compared to others.

Burial Insurance for Sleep Apnea

A lot of funeral insurance providers find a way to make mention of a medical condition such as sleep apnea in their questionnaires. But how they describe it is what matters.

Getting the perfect burial insurance with a pre-existing medical condition such as sleep apnea is very important. Also, finding the right agent is just as necessary.

Health Questions

In most instances, an insurance company will mention sleep apnea in the following ways.

- In the last 2 years, have you had this condition? Did a doctor diagnose you with the condition? Or have you received medical treatment for sleep apnea?

- Over the past two years, have made use of oxygen equipment to help you with sleeping (excluding use for sleep apnea)?

It is very rare for an insurance company to ask directly about sleep apnea. Most funeral insurance companies are fine with an applicant who has sleep apnea.

What You Should Expect

If you encounter a lesser company, you may be required to pay a higher amount for your burial insurance as a result of this medical disorder. But a good agency should make sure you qualify for coverage immediately, at an affordable amount.

When it comes to getting burial insurance, having this disorder is just like not having. This is because a lot of insurance carriers don't care if you have sleep apnea or not.

Using Oxygen and/or CPAP

Every burial insurance company will ask if you use oxygen equipment for breathing. If you do, you will immediately become ineligible for coverage.

The exception is for sleep apnea. Mostly, the insurance company will mention that sleep apnea is the one condition where they are accepting of oxygen use.

How to Get a Good Burial Insurance with Sleep Apnea

By now, you should know that sleep apnea will not cause any problems. Finding the best and most affordable burial insurance can be an easy process. Keep in mind that the best burial insurance is just the one that protects you immediately and is the cheapest.

You might have trouble finding the best burial insurance coverage plan for sleep apnea when you mistakenly work with an insurance company that has no experience. An experienced insurance agency should provide you with a simplified coverage plan for this disorder.

Some qualities to look out for include:

- The insurance agency should be perfectly fine with sleep apnea and oxygen use due to the condition.

- The company having the least monthly coverage for sleep apnea.

- The policy should have the highest benefit payment that can protect you immediately.

The Most Affordable Burial Insurance with Oxygen Guaranteed

If you or your loved one is on oxygen, you will probably need to get information about burial insurance for people on oxygen. Usually, those who require oxygen supplement for their daily lives have a serious medical condition and wonder how to get burial insurance on oxygen.

People that have experienced a health crisis mostly consider how their loved ones will survive with the monetary burden and other expenses. You need good burial insurance that promises to give your family peace of mind.

An insurance provider will ask about oxygen use in the application. Shopping for funeral insurance on oxygen can be very difficult and frustrating, particularly if you talk to the wrong insurance company. Although oxygen use might be considered uninsurable, it is possible to get funeral insurance when you're on oxygen.

Who Needs to be on Oxygen?

Oxygen is vital for our existence. We need oxygen for normal body function. Without sufficient oxygen, the body gets weak, which results to stress and can even be dangerous if it happens for a long period.

Some symptoms of insufficient supply of oxygen include rapid heart rate, shortness of breath, confusion, and bluish skin on the nose, lips, or fingernails. People with breathing disorders cannot get sufficient oxygen naturally; they need oxygen therapy.

Supplementary oxygen is a therapy ordered by a doctor that gives extra oxygen to support important bodily functions. Oxygen therapy will make it possible for you to take in higher concentrations of oxygen than non-supplemental oxygen users.

Insufficient oxygen supply can be caused by lung conditions preventing the lungs from absorbing oxygen, such as:

- Cystic fibrosis
- Heart failure
- Pneumonia
- Sleep apnea
- Asthma
- Chronic Obstructive Pulmonary Disease (COPD)
- Bronchopulmonary dysplasia
- Chronic bronchitis
- Respiratory system trauma

When Does a Person Need Supplemental Oxygen?

To decide if a person needs oxygen therapy, doctors have to test the amount of oxygen in the arterial blood. Low levels suggest that you need supplemental oxygen. Normal levels of blood oxygen should be between 75 and 100 mmHg. A level of 60 mmHg or less requires oxygen therapy.

Oxygen requirement varies depending on how severe the lung disease is. Some people need oxygen therapy when they get ill, others having sleep apnea may only require supplementary oxygen while sleeping at night. However, people having severe conditions might require supplemental oxygen use throughout the day.

A person needs stick to the instructions of their doctor when using supplementary oxygen. If you're supposed to use additional oxygen all day, and you always forget to do so, you are putting yourself in danger of having a low oxygen level; this can cause a serious medical emergency.

If you or your loved one is on oxygen, you will probably need to get information about burial insurance for people on oxygen. Usually, those who require oxygen supplement for their daily lives have a serious medical condition.

People that have experienced a health crisis mostly consider how their loved ones would survive with the financial requirements of the funeral and other expenses. You need good funeral insurance that will not be much of a hassle for your family.

An insurance provider will ask about oxygen use in the application. Shopping for funeral insurance on oxygen can be very difficult and frustrating, particularly if you talk to the wrong insurance company. Although oxygen use might be considered uninsurable, it is possible to get funeral insurance when you're on oxygen.

Eligibility for Oxygen Burial Insurance

Those on oxygen therapy mostly have a serious medical condition, probably heart or lung conditions that prevent the lungs from absorbing sufficient oxygen. People who have experienced such a health crisis may be wondering how buying burial insurance when on oxygen works.

When getting funeral insurance when on oxygen, you'll need to answer some questions in your application. You are required to provide your basic information and answer medical history questions with a YES or a NO. This makes it possible for the application to be processed quickly and easily.

But you need to take note that not all applications for burial insurance on oxygen are the same. You need to understand the processes. Some question formats include:

- Do you presently make use of oxygen daily?

- Have you used supplementary oxygen in the last 6 months for any reason?

- In the past 1 year, have you used oxygen because of a serious medical condition?

Getting Burial Insurance When on Oxygen Treatment

Whether your doctor refers to your oxygen use as therapeutic or supplemental, you probably need it to stay healthy. Doctors offer oxygen prescription because a person might have a condition preventing him or her from getting sufficient oxygen through normal respiration.

Your medical provide likely had you go for a blood draw to determine the amount of oxygen in your blood. He or she might also use a pulse meter to determine oxygen levels. If you show symptoms of low oxygen, the doctor will probably put you on oxygen therapy.

They will provide you with portable liquid oxygen tanks, oxygen gas tanks, or a concentrator that creates it for you from the air around you. You might make use of a nasal cannula, a continuous positive airway pressure device, or a mask to receive it.

There are several benefits to using oxygen therapy, and for most, they are life-saving advantages. Although you may not get your need for oxygen much difficult, there are likely other problems linked to it that can be frustrating.

This process can be challenging for most people, and it is because a lot of insurance companies are not willing to provide coverage to people with many kinds of health impairments.

The Bottom Line When It Comes to Oxygen

Every life insurance company will unequivocally ask about your oxygen use. There is only one possible outcome where you can get a level death benefit while using supplementary oxygen.

Burial Insurance Underwriting on Oxygen

All funeral insurance companies will have health questions and a check on your prescription history. They need this information to determine if you are eligible or not. Their questionnaires will have various parts for different health conditions.

How to Get Good Burial Insurance on Oxygen

If you are on oxygen, you have several levels of death benefit options. To get good burial insurance on oxygen, work with an independent brokerage that represents various insurance companies. This agency will look for an insurance company that will provide the best price.

High-Risk Burial Insurance on Oxygen

There are serious carriers that issue out "high-risk health issue" burial insurance. They provide insurance for most health conditions, and many can have a policy ready the same day you request for coverage.

These companies specialize in coverage for those with some common conditions, including people using oxygen due to pre-existing conditions. However, there are some carriers who will not ask clients to take a medical exam, but will need clear answers to some health questions, before providing a quote.

Can You Get Funeral Insurance on Your Parents?

As a benefactor, if you are eager to get insurance coverage because a parent or loved one has given you the duty of taking care of them, there are things you can do with them to get insurance coverage with reputable burial insurance company.

With the average costs of a funeral increasing, it will be best to look for ways to spare your family the stress and troubles of scrambling to get funds, or worse, paying for it over time at a high-interest rate.

LIFE INSURANCE FOR MULTIPLE SCLEROSIS: BEST COMPANIES AND RATES

To qualify for affordable life insurance for multiple sclerosis hinges on your life insurance carrier and the severity of the MS. Multiple sclerosis is considered a high-risk life insurance policy. Though, you can still get does not mean that you cannot get approval at adequate premiums. In this article, we introduce:

• MS Life coverage

• Prices and how to qualify for life coverage with MS

• Types of life coverage and multiple sclerosis

• What information does an insurance agent need to know regarding your Multiple Sclerosis?

• How to apply for multiple sclerosis life insurances

• Are you refusing to take out life insurance for multiple sclerosis?

• Life insurance companies with favorable multiple sclerosis

Life Insurance is Not Exciting. Let's Get Down to the Basis! Here are the Main Conclusions.

You can obtain Multiple sclerosis life insurances. It depends on whether your MS is unique or suspicious. You can assume that you will receive a life insurance approval through MS between the standard and table 4 rating.

MS Life Insurance (Multiple Sclerosis)

It can be a boring process to find a Multiple Sclerosis life insurance.

There are too many types of policies to choose from, and thousands of companies claim they have "the most suitable policy for you." The issue now is determining how to choose between these highly rated companies, especially with a prior situation like Multiple Sclerosis.

Can You Get Life Insurance for Multiple Sclerosis?

Well. You need to use the right life insurance company to get affordable life insurance with MS. If you need MS life insurance, and you were recently denied life insurance or received an offer far above your expectations, you've come to the right place. For many years we have been helping consumers find affordable life insurance with MS. When searching for term life insurance for people with MS, there are a few important things to keep in mind.

Life Insurance Rates and Multiple Sclerosis Eligibility

You need to understand the following health categories to understand our idea here:

Multiple Sclerosis and Health Categories

There are 12 health categories:

- Preferred Best

- Preferred

- Standard Plus

- Standard

- Preferred Smoker

- Smoker

- Table 1-12

Experience has shown that you add 25% to the standard fee for each table rating. Most companies reject underwriting after table 8. Most applicants for multiple sclerosis control meet the health level requirements of Table 4, which means the rate is double the standard rates. If Standard is $50/month, Table 4 would $100 / month. Table 5 is $125/month. Table 6 would be $ 150 / month, etc. Now, let's look at how to qualify for life insurance with a specific MS.

What Type of MS Do You Have? Suspected" or "Definite"

If multiple sclerosis is suspected, MS's attack is present, but no test results are available to support the diagnosis. There are no signs of illness and no recommended treatments.

The best option for MS:

• Within three to four years of the attack: Table 2

• Within two years of the attack: Table 3

• After four years: Standard

Definite MS means you've had at least two attacks and received test results to support the diagnosis. Of course, Definite MS can also include anyone who has been recommended for treatment and has a disorder, as it affects the time you spend walking. The best option for Definite MS:

• Within two years since the last attack: Table 7

• 3-5 years since your last attack: Table 5

• 6-10 years since the last attack: Table 3

• More than ten years since the last attack: Standard

If the severity exceeds the minimum, the ratings will increase, and it's possible for your underwriting to be declined if the case is severe. Please note that if you have an acute exacerbation or immunosuppressive disease, the life insurance company will take back their offer until the disease is treated.

Types of Multiple Sclerosis and Life Insurance

The type **of** multiple sclerosis you have will determine your rate.

There are four types of MS:

Relapse-remitting MS (RRMS): It is the most common MS. It is the easiest MS to insure because of its transient MS period called a flare-ups or relapse.

Secondary Progressive MS (SPMS): You can insure it, but the best-case scenario is shown in Table 3. Most of the cases we've seen fall within the scope of Table 4-6.

Primary Progressive MS (PPMS): Sometimes, it can be insured, but coverage is usually declined.

Progressive MS (PRMS): Usually, the coverage is always decline.

The points above are general rules. If you don't fall into that particular category, you shouldn't be discouraged from applying for life insurance. This disease affects everyone differently. It is, therefore, necessary that you provide the agent with the details of the MS.

What Does Your Life Insurance Agent Need to Know About MS?

We don't expect you to understand all the information we have provided.

Here is a list of important information that agents can use to determine which insurance company will best treat your MS favorably:

- Age of diagnosis

- Number of attacks and date of the last attack

- Any medication currently being taken MS diagnosis (see description above)

- Is the nervous system damaged? No damage? Minimal / medium / severe residual disorder?

- Other health problems?

Pro tip: If your agent did not ask you this question, find another one. They don't have enough experience to find the best rate for you.

Using the above information, many agents ask a common question:

Do you have mild, moderate, or severe MS?

They ask this question to know whether you qualify for fully underwritten coverage. If your MS is severe, you are not qualified for fully underwritten coverage and will advise you to take guaranteed issue life coverage products.

- **Mild:** Fewer seizures, long remission time, and no disability.

- **Moderate**: Increased frequency/duration with some residual neurological disorders, but you feel fine.

- **Severe:** Can only sit in a wheelchair or lie on a bed and needs help with daily activities.

They ask this because when the situation is severe, they know you are not eligible for fully comprehensive insurance, and they can advise you to subscribe to life insurance products.

How to Apply for MS Life Insurance

In the absence of MS underwriting experience, new life insurance agents spread many myths. They saw a case, went to the wrong life insurance company, and limit their knowledge from a single experience. After helping many consumers qualify to get MS life insurance, here are some key points based on our years of experience.

Fact 1: You can get standard rates (term insurance or life insurance). When MS has relapse, remission, and there is enough time.

Fact 2: No two insurance carriers will case similarly. They all see your MS differently. While some companies decline you, another company might offer you affordable rates. Each life insurance policy covers multiple sclerosis differently.

Fact 3: Independent agents have the greatest chance of bringing you the cheapest rates. They will compare the market and subscription guidelines to ensure the best rate for you. Most of the life insurance agents out there have limited knowledge. They only offer one company.

Has Your Application for Multiple Sclerosis Life Insurance Been Declined?

Don't let a past decline for life insurance discourage you from searching for new insurance. If you are sure your MS is under control, your agent may have selected the wrong operator.

If your MS is severe, you are not eligible for life insurance; you can choose a different insurance policy. For those who are not eligible for term life insurance for multiple sclerosis, a graded death benefit life insurance policy is a popular option with a 2-year waiting period before the full insurance premium can be paid. There are also accidental policies that only pay out on accidents option. To get life insurance for multiple sclerosis, you need an experienced agent to underwrite your risk. A seasoned life insurance agent will understand how to place your MS more profitably for insurers and know which company has the most liberal underwriting guidelines for patients with multiple sclerosis.

Life Insurance Company with Multiple Sclerosis Underwriting

Currently, we look for the best deals with AIG and American National for universal life insurance and traditional term life insurance. Sometimes, we do have good deals with Prosperity insurance. Remember, you need an experienced agent to get a favorable health classification (which ultimately means a better rate). A skilled agent can write an exciting cover letter that will explain your risks and highlight your MS diagnosis and lifestyle motivation.

Best Burial Insurance Company with Multiple Sclerosis

Suppose you are looking for a whole life insurance policy (with an insured amount of $5, 000 to $30,000), commonly known as burial Insurance, Final Expense Insurance, or Funeral Insurance. In that case, the aim is to be eligible for the first-day coverage without waiting two years to receive benefits. Most burial insurance has classified MS. Sentinel Security, the best life insurance company, did not require a waiting period. It will interest you to know that they have some of the cheapest rates for this type of life insurance on the market. No medical examination is required, and you will receive a decision while on the phone. Sometimes, your coverage can begin within 30 minutes.

Bottom Line

It might be challenging to get life insurance with MS, but we can help. At Superior Mutual, we have helped MS patients get life insurance times without numbers. This is, of course, possible, and we are always available to assist you in getting a coverage for you and your family. There are several options, and in some cases, the possibilities are very affordable. Kindly fill the form below, and an experienced independent life insurance agent will gather the necessary information required and advise you on the best eligible option.

Discover the Lowest Cost Burial Insurance with Scleroderma

As an applicant with Scleroderma, obtaining approval for life insurance can be daunting.

Some of our clients had narrated their horrible experience while trying to secure insurance coverage, and it shouldn't be that way if you work with a qualified and experienced agency that works with riskier life insurance.

We help more people get affordable scleroderma life insurance, and below is the summary of what you should be expecting in this article.

- Life Insurance with Scleroderma

- The expected rates for you as an applicant with Scleroderma

- Case Studies of Life insurance with Scleroderma

- In conclusion, obtaining life insurance is a possibility

Here Are the Few Things to Note Ahead

To get approved as a scleroderma patient for life insurance, the life insurer wants to confirm that Scleroderma has only affected local areas, such as the hands and face, and that Scleroderma is not moving too fast.

Life Insurance with Scleroderma

Scleroderma is very favorable for life insurance risks when it only affects the skin of the hands and face and progress slowly.

It does not spread fast and does not have severe complications.

Difficult life insurance cases for Scleroderma are called Limit Disease, which is also known as CREST syndrome.

A lot of companies will deny you insurance coverage for Scleroderma, but we can get coverage in most of these cases, which will be explained below.

You will have difficulty getting life insurance coverage if the Scleroderma is systemic and affects large parts of your skin and organs.

You are likely to get the best offer if you are someone who:

- Is very active.

- Does not smoke.

- Avoid a diet that can trigger heartburn.

- Does not expose skin to cold.

The information below will be used in giving you a quote. Always avoid agents that would not ask questions like this from you. Agents who do not remember to inquire about these things are only guessing, and the rates that will be offered will only be to make money from you without them truly knowing the option that suits your situation.

- Smoking Status.

- When you were diagnosed.

- The scleroderma type and the part of the body affected.

- Medications or treatment being taken.

- Treatments and drugs that you have taken.

- Any evidence of progression?

- The test result, whether Pulmonary or EKG.

- Any other health conditions?

The Expected Rates for You as an Applicant with Scleroderma

Before knowing those things, you need to expect, you need to see the table ratings for life insurance.

This is an additional fee to the standard rate.

Usually, the tables are about 25% more expensive. Therefore, in table 2 rates, you should expect standard rates + 50% while table 4 is Standard Rates + 100%.

Do you now understand?

That being said, below is what you should expect for life insurance with Scleroderma when it comes to pricing.

The best case would be the localized Scleroderma; it is likely to be in Table 2. You can't get preferred rates if you have Scleroderma.

CREST Scleroderma will be at least on Table 4, and possibly a decline under severe circumstances.

For localized and CREST scleroderma, if you take any steroids or immunosuppressive medications, then there will be an additional two tables to your rating.

If you are for a traditional insurer, automatically, you will be getting a decline for Diffuse systemic disease; however, we can offer you graded benefits.

If your Scleroderma has nothing to do with skin and only involves the organ, you will be getting declined by the traditional insurer. We also have graded death benefit policies in this regard.

Case Studies of Life insurance with Scleroderma

Case Study #1

A Male non-smoker, Age 58. He has Scleroderma diagnosis in the past eight years. Involves only the skin. There was no complications or a sign of progression. The documentation of favorable testing was consistent.

Through us, he was able to secure Standard rates with many insurers.

Case Study #2

A female non-smoker, Age 50. Has her CREST diagnosis in the last 13 months. Not progressive, mild, and no internal organs were involved. There was no treatment needed except the acid reflux treatment.

Initially, she got declined before working with us. And we were able to get a Table 3 rating, which she was happy about.

Guaranteed Acceptance Life Insurance is Always the Last Resort for Scleroderma

If your Scleroderma has progressed faster or affected more severe areas, as opposed to your hands or face, you may have difficulty obtaining approval for a traditional life insurance plan.

While this can be scary or leave you helpless, you must know there are many other options to consider for life insurance coverage.

Undoubtedly, the most common type of life insurance to consider when you are unable to obtain a life insurance coverage is guaranteed acceptance life insurance.

The policy does not require a medical examination, and your Scleroderma does not want to have any effect on your approvals.

As an alternative to a waiting period of 24 months for your insurance policy to be fully functional, you will not be asked any questions.

The coverage will typically be between $5,000 and $35,000 and, after the 24 months, your coverage will be fully functional and will work like any other life insurance policy.

Usually, we recommend companies like AIG, Gerber Life, or Sons of Norway Insurance Company if you want to go with this option.

In Conclusion, Obtaining Life Insurance is a Possibility

We have worked with many applicants with Scleroderma; therefore, we know which insurer will accept the risk.

When you apply for an insurance coverage with Scleroderma, it is essential to work with an agency that has experienced when it comes to underwriting cases like this and with an agency that has several life insurers option for you.

The tips mentioned above will provide you with the best chance of getting approval for coverage at the most affordable price.

We appreciate you allowing us to assess your risk, and you can be assured that we will offer the best offers available.

HOW TO GET AFFORDABLE RATES FOR BURIAL INSURANCE IF YOU HAVE EPILEPSY

Getting affordable life insurance for epilepsy and seizures is difficult for some people; however, it should not always be if you reach out to the right agency.

We usually find that people with epilepsy do not have life insurance coverage or pay exaggerated premiums because they choose the wrong agency to work for, leading to the wrong insurers.

Whenever you request coverage for conditions such as epilepsy, you must offer yourself many options and many excellent life insurance companies.

We are a specialist in helping people search the best life insurance rates for people with epilepsy.

Here Are Two Fascinating Facts

- Whether your health is good or bad, we can help you obtain insurance coverage. We can get a policy for anyone. Remember, we will work hard to find what works best for you.

- Funeral insurance never needs to undergo any physical or medical examination. Also, you will not have to provide your doctor's files. It's just a health question. In some cases, there won't be health questions.

Epilepsy is a life-changing condition that affects a lot of Americans. We're delighted to be able to provide these people affordable funeral life insurance. Reach out to us, and we can also assist you.

Understanding Life Insurance for Epilepsy

As I mentioned earlier, your life insurance for epilepsy can be approved if you work with the correct agencies and select the appropriate company to offer insurance coverage.

What is expected of you to know is that if you are presently showing the symptoms of epilepsy, you know very well that you are approved for coverage at standard rates. Typically, it means you fall into the third-best health and pricing class available from almost all life insurers.

Epilepsy is a Well-Known Health Problem

It is one of the five most typical neurological disorders that can affect people of any age group.

Life insurers have a good knowledge of this and understand that there are excellent treatments and medications.

Also, they understand that it is still possible to lead a healthy life with epilepsy.

All you have to do is understand the process of underwriting and find the best company, and you are good to go.

Underwriting Life Insurance for People with Epilepsy

Because of the high percentage of deaths from accidents due to seizures, rather than the episodes themselves, underwriters put more focus on the frequency and severity of seizures than on the particular type of attacks diagnosed.

If you have managed to control epilepsy, you know that you will have an everyday life. Some people who have epilepsy have been rejected or have very high insurance premiums.

If you fall into this category, then you should read this article down to the end.

If you search for life insurance and have epilepsy or seizures, the important thing is to find a company that considers the case favorably.

Most of the agents don't know the right thing to ask or which company to choose to be sincere. However, we do.

As agents, we offer life insurance for epilepsy or seizures at very reasonable rates, and we do this frequently.

You need an experienced agent to underwrite this risk and know at what price life insurers charge the highest rates for people with epilepsy.

The Health Questions

The first thing is the legal questions on health. They are always simple, requiring yes or no. Your responses to them will determine your options.

Several health questions come up when it comes to epilepsy. You will be required to pay special attention to problems related to the following topics:

- Epilepsy itself

- Home health care

- Requiring assistance with daily living activities, e.g., dressing, eating, medication, bathing, taking medication, and toileting.

- Wheelchair usage

- Seizures

- Neurological conditions

Epilepsy Medications

Besides the questions about your health, they will also review your medication history. Because medications are commonly used to treat epilepsy, funeral insurers know which ones to check. Here is a list of widely labeled drugs for epilepsy. If you take them, most companies will treat you as an epilepsy patient, no matter what response you gave to your health questions.

Two things to remember.

Don't worry if you don't have epilepsy and are taking any of these medications. Many companies will not impose a penalty on you for this if you do not have epilepsy.

If we contact one of the companies that accept patients with epilepsy, none of these medications will be an issue.

- Carbamazepine
- Clonazepam
- Diazepam
- Eslicarbazepine
- Ethosuximide
- Felbamate
- Lamotrigine
- Levetiracetam
- Lorazepam (Ativan)
- Locasamide (VIMPAT)
- Oxcarbazepine (Oxtellar XR, Trileptal)
- Perampanel (Fycompa)

- Phenobarbitol
- Pregabalin (Lyrica)
- Phenytoin (Dilantin)
- Topiramate (Topamax)
- Tiagabine (Gabitril)
- Valproate (Depakene, Depakote)
- Zonisamide (Zonegran)

There may be other medications for recurrent seizures that they have labeled; however, this summarizes most of them.

The Options You Should Expect

When you have epilepsy, insurers will provide one of the four responses listed below. Each funeral insurer has a different has special underwriting, so each responds individually.

Companies with No Response

There are life insurance companies available out there that are perfectly okay with epilepsy. They will levy the same rate on an applicant who is in perfect health and has no condition whatsoever. However, we hope you have no other health problems that can prevent you from being eligible for these companies.

You Will Be Offered a Modified Plan

Typically, this type of plan has an entire waiting period of two years, and you will be charged 30 to 100% more premium. To be sincere, you do not have a reason to go for a plan from a company that offers this as it would be much cheaper to get a guaranteed issue policy without any health concerns.

It will also have a waiting period of two years, but it will be much cheaper. You pay only 15-40% more, which is significantly less.

You Will be Offered a Graded Plan

They usually cost 15-50% more; however, they also offer some instant protection. They generally pay 30-40% of the benefit if you die with the first 12 months. They will also pay 70-80% of the benefit if you die away within the second year of the insurance.

After two years, you will be completely protected for a lifetime.

You Will Be Rejected

Some insurance companies will indeed reject you if you have epilepsy. Some insurers are reluctant to take on this type of risk.

Other Options for You as an Applicant with Epilepsy

Now, for a moment, probably for a second, let us make an assumption that you have less control over your epilepsy or have recently been hospitalized or disabled.

You may have been denied life insurance and need to consider some other options.

In this case, you should discuss the use of products like guaranteed issue life insurance with your agent. With these products, you do not need to complete health questions, but several related conditions apply.

However, companies like Sons of Norway and Gerber offer excellent products that can get the ball rolling and start protecting you and your family.

DISCOVER THE PATH TO AFFORDABLE BURIAL INSURANCE WITH HEPATITIS

Treatment of Hepatitis A and Hepatitis B is a reality for many people. Hepatitis C no longer carries the "death sentence" title. Modern-day medicine is incredible.

Some insurance companies are still reluctant to cover hepatitis patients. Yet, we work hand in hand with insurance companies that provide a final expense plan (also called a burial plan) for Hepatitis.

Let's explore the necessary steps and what to expect regarding qualifying for Final Expense Insurance if you have had or do have Hepatitis.

Underwriting Process

The level policy of an insurance company is the policy with the lowest rates and immediate coverage. To qualify for the level policy, the green light through the underwriting process is necessary. We'll take a look at what to expect from the underwriting process if you have Hepatitis.

The underwriting process clarifies answers to basic medical questions. It is the process of evaluating your level of risk. The problems within this process vary by the insurance company. While the questions differ, the goal of the underwriting process remains the same. They want to check out your medical history.

Insurance companies then determine how you fit with a plan according to their guidelines and understanding. Be aware of the wording insurance companies use in the underwriting process. Some companies will refer to Hepatitis as "liver disease."

Time also plays a huge factor. Insurance companies took into account when you discovered Hepatitis and how long you've had it for. These time-sensitive questions allow them to make better judgment calls on what type of treatment you need.

Example questions:

- **When were you diagnosed with Hepatitis? Which type?**

- **Have you ever experienced any liver disease?**

- **In the last two years, were you treated for Hepatitis?**

When it comes to underwriting Hepatitis C, there is a more in-depth assessment. This assessment evaluates factors such as liver damage, laboratory results, and any treatments that have been distributed. Within the underwriting process, insurance companies will ask about medications and medication history. They use this medication history to categorize users as high or low risk.

If you take any hepatitis medications, insurance companies will flag you for risk assessment. Insurance companies will find out if you are on one of these medications, so we need to understand what medications you are on. These are common Hepatitis medications they look out for:

- Adefovir Dipivoxil (Hepsera)
- Boceprevir
- Daclatasvir and sofosbuvir (Daklinza)
- Dasabuvir-ombitasvir-paritaprevir-ritonavir (Viekira Pak)
- Elbasvir-grazoprevir (Zepatier)
- Entecavir (Baraclude)

- Glecaprevir-pibrentasvir (Mavyret)
- Incivek
- Infergen
- Interferon Alfacon
- Intron-A
- Lamivudine (Epivir-HBV, Zeffix, or Heptodin)
- Ledipasvir-sofosbuvir (Harvoni)
- Olysio
- Ombitasvir
- Ombitasvir-paritaprevir-ritonavir (Technivie)
- Pegasys
- Rebetron
- Ribasphere
- Ribavirin
- Roferon
- Simeprevir
- Sofosbuvir and velpatasvir (Epclusa)
- Sofosbuvir-velpatasvir-voxilaprevir (Vosevi)
- Sovaldi
- Telaprevir
- Tenofovir disoproxil (Viread)
- Victrelis
- Zepatier

Currently, Hepatitis C has no effective vaccine. But, with advancements in modern medicine, there are treatments available. Unlike Hepatitis A and B, which are commonly found with an infection, Hepatitis C is often detected after being in the body's system for an extended period.

Because Hepatitis C is a high risk, most insurance companies will offer coverage at a higher cost. This higher cost is a jump of 35-50% more than the preferred plan on monthly rates. Again, this depends on the insurance company and the underwriting process.

Burial Insurance Common Coverage

After the underwriting process, the insurance company should know precisely what they can offer you based on your needs.

Here are some possible outcomes you could experience based on your medical history and current needs:

You've had Hepatitis C Within the Last Two Years

- Higher Premium

- Final Expense Insurance Plan

If you fall into this category, we represent Liberty Bankers Life, an insurance company that offers a coverage plan at a low cost with immediate protection. They offer a policy that pays full death benefits starting the very first day.

If you do not qualify for Liberty Bankers Life, your coverage policy might be a little costly. Your benefit payments may not begin until the first two years.

These plans are "graded plans" meaning if you pass away 30-40% of your death benefits pay out the first year, and 70-80% the second year. Graded plans are the most common among insurance companies for Hepatitis patients.

You had Hepatitis C Over Two Years Ago

- Lower Premium

- Level Death Benefit Eligibility

Some Burial Insurance Plans ask about Hepatitis C within the last two years. Since this would not apply to you, eligibility for a Level Death Benefit comes into play. A Level Death Benefit protects you immediately while lowering the insurance rate for coverage.

You've had Hepatitis A or B Within the Last Year

- Lower Premium

- Level Death Benefit Eligibility

Because advancements in medicine have discovered effective vaccines, recovery from Hepatitis A or B is widespread. Most insurance companies only ask about Hepatitis C. You're looking at qualifying for a Level Death Benefit if you've had Hepatitis A or B. Our objective is to match you up with the best possible coverage plan to prepare for future success.

THE REALITY OF BURIAL INSURANCE FOR AN APPLICANT WITH HIV OR AIDS

Is it possible to get funeral insurance as an HIV patient? Usually, you might think conditions such as HIV or AIDS will prevent you from getting the coverage you need.

So, the Truth is;

It does not matter whether you have HIV; you can still get burial insurance. But you will have to go through a compulsory waiting period of two years before the total death benefit can be released.

If you are surprised by this, then you should know you are not alone. A lot of people approach us with the same understanding. We have assisted many people in obtaining affordable life insurance, even though they had HIV. It's really very simple, and we will let you know how simple the process is. It may come as a surprise, but you can get affordable funeral insurance for health problems!

In this article, we will show you the options available to you if you have been diagnosed with HIV or AIDS. Also, we will teach you how to get the best funeral policy at an affordable price. There is no funeral insurer that provides policy with underwriting that will accept a candidate with AIDS or HIV. Therefore, the only way to get a policy is to go for a guarantee issue life option. These plans have certain conditions which we will review extensively. The great news is that getting a policy is possible.

Here is Good News for You

You will never have to undergo a physical or medical examination. You do not even need to provide medical records. The registration process only requires you to answer a few questions.

HIV and AIDS are definitely reducing your life insurance options. Thank God, some doors are still open for you; therefore, you can rest easy and discover that your final expenses will not burden your loved ones.

Funeral Insurance for HIV patients

Can you be refused burial insurance as an HIV patient? Nowadays, many things are changing very fast both in insurance and the people's quest to find treatment for conditions like HIV/AIDS. For anyone worried about the Burial insurance coverage, more options than ever before are now available.

Knowing Burial Insurance Coverage

What is the cost of burial insurance? It does not matter the name you give it, final expense or burial insurance coverage, you're still saying the same thing. It is simply an insurance plan purchased to cover the cost of the funeral for a loved one to pay for a life event like this, you might be surprised to learn that an average funeral costs around $7,000; however, it can even exceed that with some thousands.

Meaning, paying for the burial can mean sinking into savings, or even managing a payment plan that extends years later.

A funeral insurance policy works like any other fixed-rate option. It is specifically paid out for expenses. Rather, you or a loved one will name a beneficiary, and they will be eligible for what was established at the time you obtained the policy.

The funds can be used for burial-related expenses like:

- Traveling for burial arrangements

- Funeral guest accommodation

- All burial expenses such as mortuary fees, casket, transportation, funeral services, and many more

- Legal costs related to the estate.

The beneficiary will receive a fixed amount and use it for these purposes. They should meet the necessities of the insurance carrier. This usually means providing a death certificate, although the carrier may ask for more while collecting the policy.

Find out What You Get with Burial Insurance.

Remember that a good funeral insurance plan can have monetary value because it is a life insurance policy that accumulates over time. Suppose you are investing at 65 and are still alive at 89. This policy probably has a cash value that you can access if you are in need of some money to help you with your medical or living expenses.

Is it similar to the plan sold in the funeral home? No. it is a prepaid funeral, and its value does not increase over time.

Instead, you will make a contract with the funeral home and pay a certain amount well before your needs, but it is not a subsistence benefit plan.

In addition, as some of the most important insurance companies cover final costs, there may be a repayment component of the plan.

That is, if you or your covered loved ones pass away during the two years of paying for the plan, you can get the policy payment back, plus an extra percentage.

Choose the Right Carrier for Burial Insurance if You Are Diagnosed With HIV/AIDS.

The source from which we purchase influences most of our buying decisions. For example, you can go to a big store to buy a cheap pair of sneakers and end up looking for another one before the year runs out.

Instead, you can go to a premium manufacturer and pay more; however, you will have more time because of that investment.

The same thing is also applicable to your funeral insurance. In fact, you will want to look for a source that will help you source information from the top-rated insurers offering funeral insurance. For example, one that directs you to insurers providing coverage to people with high-risk health problems.

Above all, HIV / AIDS can be an extremely treated condition nowadays, but it is still considered a health deficit with a very high risk for an insurance company.

Not all funeral insurance will willingly offer coverage or may require huge sums to extend a plan. However, some niche insurance providers are willing to work with clients experiencing some of the worst health problems, including those living with HIV.

They will not ask you to undergo a rigorous medical examination before offering you a plan. Instead, they will examine a few basic medical questions (most of them with yes or no answers) and then provide a set of quotes.

This will vary depending on your diagnosis, general health, your age, and perhaps even several factors related to your medication.

Can I Obtain a Burial Policy If HIV/AIDS is Not Controlled?

Yes, but….

Guaranteed Issue Life Insurance Is Your Only Option

As you are not eligible for a plan with an underwriting, the only way to guarantee coverage is through a policy without health questions. They are often called guaranteed issue or guaranteed acceptance.

These types of funeral policies do not raise health problems or consider your health history. Literally, they issue policy blindly. In as much as you have the age and sound mind to sign a legal contract, you have permission.

The Guaranteed acceptance of burial insurance policies is still life insurance. This means that the monthly premiums will be paid for life, the plan lasts forever, and the benefits cannot be reduced.

Disadvantages of Guaranteed Issue

- Final insurance with a guaranteed issue has two main disadvantages.

- It has higher premiums than other plans with health questions.

- A compulsory minimum waiting period of two years

As you might have known, the premiums are much higher. The risk assumed by the insurer is much higher because they do not know about the health of an applicant. As a result, they must charge higher premiums to compensate for this increased risk.

The two-year waiting period is necessary to avoid the application from people closer to passing away. Insurance companies would be quickly destroyed financially without this clause.

Within the waiting period, they will reimburse all premiums with interest if you die. After the 2-year of waiting, you will be completely protected instantly.

Advantages of Guaranteed Issue

Everything has it's good and bad. The most apparent benefit that your coverage is guaranteed. Most people living with HIV or AIDS will stop seeking coverage after accessing numerous companies, and they are being denied. If only applicants knew about these plans without health questions. Thank Goodness they are available. It is incredible for people in certain selected health situations like this. The application is straightforward. Primarily, you just need to provide your personal information together with the recipients and payment information, and that's it. It only takes a few minutes.

Discover the Path to Affordable Burial Insurance with Parkinson's Disease

Usually, you might think that getting funeral insurance for Parkinson's disease would be very difficult and expensive; however, you would be wrong. Even if you have Parkinson's disease, funeral insurance at the lowest cost with immediate coverage is possible. Over the years, we have helped many people with this neurological condition to get good funeral insurance at the most affordable cost possible.

And We Can Also Definitely Help You!

Please read to understand how the Burial insurance company responds to applicants with conditions like Parkinson's disease. Also, the various kind of insurance plans that you can expect from these companies.

Most importantly, you should know that we can help you get the highest quality and affordable burial insurance, no matter how serious.

Insurance companies can provide affordable plans because they understand that even though Parkinson's disease cannot be cured, medications can be used to control the symptoms. Like other conditions such as systemic lupus, multiple sclerosis, etc.

There are also many different complementary therapies that are used in conjunction with traditional medicine to help people live healthy lives with this lifelong neurological disorder.

Note: If you have been prescribed to use cannabis by-products to help you control Parkinson's disease symptoms, this might lead to some questions from some state-owned insurance companies that might see the use of marijuana for medication as being illegal.

This is one of many situations where the help of professional and experienced funeral insurance specialists will be necessary to help you avoid penalty or, worse, getting declined.

There are some top-level Funeral insurance companies that we have access to, and they can also provide an insurance plan at the most affordable rates with instant total benefit coverage from the first day. This type of burial plan is called level, simplified, or preferred by insurance companies.

In order to ascertain your eligibility for the level insurance plan, you need to undergo an underwriting process for the insurer to identify whether you have other health issues that might be a concern to them.

The level burial insurance is usually provided to a healthy individual or people who have no health problems considered high risk.

Some of these major burial insurance companies that are okay with an applicant with Parkinson's disease will provide a level plan unless the applicant has a serious illness or other medical condition that has been red-flagged by them.

In addition, unlike other life insurance, you do not have to go through all the troubles to prepare for medical exams like physical, blood tests, EKGs, urine tests, etc. before you can apply for funeral insurance or closing expenses.

You can apply for final expense insurance for Parkinson's disease or any health issue right from the comfort of your home through a phone call to your funeral insurance agent or agency.

We are pleased to report that some of the final expense companies are not concerned about Parkinson's disease. To them, having the disease does not change anything. You are entitled to death benefits as others. This means that you can pay the minimum amount, and there is no waiting period for coverage.

Although most burial insurance imposes a penalty on patients with Parkinson's disease, at the very least, the premium will be higher, and the waiting period is more extended; however, it is also dependent on the company. Another important thing is not having any ailments that can disqualify you from carriers that accept PD.

Ready for More Good News?

Since funeral insurance policies are simplified, they do not require any medical examination. A stranger does not have to enter your home once registration is complete.

Parkinson's disease is incurable, and it can be harmful to your life. Thanks to contemporary treatment that has allowed many people to live a longer with better quality of life. Irrespective of your condition, we are fully confident that we can provide you with a very reasonable funeral insurance policy.

NOTE: you can't buy burial insurance directly from almost every company, especially those with lower premiums. If you call the insurance company directly and inquire about the process of applying for the coverage, they will simply direct you to their agent to purchase their insurance policies.

The Bad News

There are many burial insurance companies that believe applicants with Parkinson's disease are very risky to deal with. Companies like these are not capable of offering a level plan for an applicant with PD.

These companies will consider accepting someone with PD as long as they charge more money to make up for what they know as very risky. There might also have a full or partial waiting period before beneficiaries are eligible for the full benefit.

To make matters worse, these companies will simply decline you, which means you would have wasted a lot of time. This is why we strongly encourage you to reach out to Final Expense insurance professionals who have access to insurers that can fully cope with Parkinson's, and you can trust us to do that.

Therefore, do not hesitate to fill out the quote form on this page or contact us for quick approval of your insurance policy at an affordable cost.

Funeral Insurance Underwriting for Parkinson's

Whether you know it or not, the only underwriting element that concerns you is the health questionnaire. Unbeknownst to you, insurers will check your prescription history to confirm your health status.

Obviously, the only way to get immediate protection and lower cost are by applying for a funeral insurance plan with underwriting. If you want to avoid health questions and medical checks, you can apply for a guarantee issue life insurance. However, this should only be the last resort after you have exhausted all underwritten options.

Parkinson's Health Questions

When applying for final expense insurance, and you are being asked questions about Parkinson's, commonly, there will not be an attached time frame. This is because the condition is incurable, and the moment you have it, you will live with it until death.

Most companies will divide their application into various sections. Generally, lifelong conditions will be in the same group. This is where you will always find Parkinson's disease. Here is an example of how they can ask questions about it.

- Have you ever been diagnosed, taken medication, or been treated for Parkinson's disease?

Some companies attach a time frame to the application, and which seems odd because the condition is incurable. However, if it happens, here is an example of how the question can be asked.

- Have you been diagnosed with Parkinson's disease or received treatment for Parkinson's disease within 24 months?

Because Parkinson's disease is a neurological condition and must be answered in yes, there are other health questions that can be answered by yes or no. You can easily answer these questions, but the best option is to consult an experienced Funeral insurance agent who can help answer for your benefit and with the right answers.

Parkinson's Medications

In addition to the health questions, insurance companies can also review your prescription records electronically. Their goal is just to check your health status. For instance, if you recently had cancer but did not disclose it, your prescription history would reveal it.

The medications below have been flagged by burial insurance companies for Parkinson's Disease. You would notice they are in category I and Category II. Category I are medications that can be used for various use. Therefore, some companies might not see as a Parkinson's patient when they are seen in your prescription record. For instance, a medication like Requip is very popular for treating restless leg syndrome. In contrast, Category II is for medications that automatically makes every funeral insurance company see you as a Parkinson's Patient. Even if you did not disclose that you are a patient, these medications in your Prescription history would do it for you.

Category I

- Akineton
- Benztropine
- Mesylate
- Cogentin
- Mirapex
- Requip
- Ropinirole
- Trihexyphenidyl HCL

Category II

- Amantadine HCL
- Apokyn
- Atamet
- Azilect
- Bromocriptine Mesylate
- Carbidopa
- Comtan
- Eldepryl
- Inbrija
- Kemadrin
- Larodopa
- Levodopa
- Lodosyn
- Neupro
- Parcopa
- Parlodel
- Pergolide Mesylate
- Permax

- Procyclidine HCL
- Selegiline HCL
- Sinemet
- Stalevo
- Symmetrel
- Tasmar
- Zelapar

Other Conditions to Consider

All patients with Parkinson's disease have a different level of symptoms and side effects. If you experience any of these problems below, you must also take that into account.

The Truth About Depression

Depression is a prevalent side effect of this condition. In most cases, doctors will prescribe medication to deal with the depression caused by Parkinson's disease.

Thankfully, many insurance companies don't pay attention to depression, even if you have a prescription or you are taking medication for it.

Daily Living Activities

When Parkinson's has gotten worse that you need someone to help you with your daily activities, it has a significant impact on the underwriting process. To be clear, insurers define daily activities like bathing, dressing, eating, using the toilet, and taking medication. They can even be shortened to ADL.

Above all, every funeral insurance companies, except Royal Neighbors of America, will inquire if you need any help with daily living activities. The point is that this carrier will also ask if you have Parkinson's. And if you have, they will include you in their graded plan, which is more expensive and offers limited benefits in the first two years.

Of course, this is better than a full waiting period; however, it is also not as good as full protection and the lowest cost. Most funeral insurance companies will decline those who need assistance in their daily activities.

If you do not qualify for the Royal Neighbors plan, your only option may be to acquire a guaranteed issue life insurance policy. This type of policy does not require health questions or medical checks. It is not very expensive but requires a two-year waiting period before death benefits are paid. If you die while waiting, all your premium plus 10% will be returned to you.

Notes: There are many devices available that can assist you in becoming independent with your activities of daily living. For example, the stabilizing spoon, if you find it hard to eat due to hand tremors.

Home Health Care

This situation equates to the need for help with daily living activities. Every burial insurance company will also ask about this. With America's royal neighbors as the only exception. If you are disqualified for some other reasons, the guaranteed acceptance policy is your only option at the time.

Some Possible Burial Insurance Underwritten Plan Offers for Parkinson's Disease Applicants

Now that you know health questions asked about this condition, the medications they are looking for, and some other situations that may affect the whole process. Here are the ways life insurers can respond to an applicant with Parkinson's.

Level Plan - Lowest Cost with Immediate Full Benefits Coverage

In fact, there are some companies that may be less interested if you have Parkinson's. Of course, there are not many of them, but they are. With them, you pay the same fee as a marathon runner. Aside from the fact that there will be no waiting period. We hope you will not be disqualified from these companies due to some other health problems.

Note: It would be best to understand that time is essential for any chronic, lifelong, or degenerative health condition such as Parkinson's disease. Therefore, you need to act now and secure funeral insurance when it is still affordable.

Graded Plan

The Graded plan for Parkinson's disease is costlier than the level plan at 20 to 50 percent. Immediately, you will be entitled to a percentage of your total death benefit in the following period:

- Year 1, starting from the first day – 40% of your total death benefit will be given to your beneficiaries.
- Year 2 – About 80% of your death benefit can be claimed by your beneficiaries.
- Year 3 - your beneficiaries can receive the full death benefit (100%) in the event of your death.

Modified plan - Highest Premium with A Full Waiting Time

This is often called a "modified" plan. The waiting period is 24 months or two years, and the monthly premium is always the highest. If you pass away at any time during the waiting period, all your premiums will be refunded at an interest rate of 10%, depending on the insurer.

Application Will Be Declined

There are many insurance companies that are not capable enough to take risks if an applicant suffers from Parkinson's disease and other common diseases associated with it. While some others will only decline you because of the condition.

Guaranteed Issue (GI) Policy Option

If you are denied the first offer (Level Plan) or the second offer and the only option you are being offered is the modified plan, your final option is the Guaranteed issue policy. The GI Policy option is not an underwritten plan, which means there won't be a need for you to answer health questions or reviews of medication history. However, the plan will be costlier and also involves a total waiting period of 2 years.

Most times, depending on the insurance company in question, the Guaranteed Issue Policy is preferable than a modified plan when it comes to quality and affordability.

On the other hand, it is much easier and convenient to contact an experienced insurance agent who has access to the country's best insurance company and who knows which one is most affordable regarding your condition.

Here is the list of the qualities that you should check for in an insurance policy and the insurance carrier offering the plan to applicants with Parkinson's diseases:

- The Insurance company must be a great option for an applicant with Parkinson's disease.
- The policy offers the highest payments that can protect you immediately, from day one, and at the lowest cost.
- The insurer may offer the best price with instant coverage, even though you need ADL assistance or home health care.

In terms of finding funeral coverage for applicants with Parkinson's disease, the insurance agency that will help you must have the following qualities:

- The insurance agency must have an insurance agent or life insurance specialist who is experienced at the funeral insurance and will also be passionate about helping you and not the company.

- In fact, the agency needs to be independent in order to have access to many of the best insurers that can offer the best rates.
- It must also be an agency that offers only the best insurance plan from Top – level insurance companies in the country that is reputable and trusted in the insurance industry with reliable finances and an excellent track record.

Why Can't You Tell Us Exactly What to Expect?

This is a good question. However, that question cannot be answered because we do not know much about you. Every funeral insurance company will do a different assessment of your health. There are a lot of variables that must be taken into consideration prior to giving an accurate and honest expectation. No one without knowing these details will be able to inform you precisely what to expect.

BURIAL INSURANCE FOR OVERWEIGHT ISSUES

It is possible to get burial insurance for overweight issues. But a lot of funeral companies have build charts that determine the weight and height of applicants that they will accept. You can qualify for insurance regulations having the least rates if you avoid providers that inquire about your weight and height.

Some insurance providers will provide great rates for overweight issues. When it comes to being on the good side, some life insurance companies are more lenient than others.

No matter your weight, you'll not have to take a medical exam if you apply to the proper insurance company. You just need to answer some questions about your general health to get the best pricing.

Unless you have severe weight-related health issues that limit your mobility, you will likely be accepted for insurance coverage. Athletes, who have a high BMI but low body fat percentage, will probably receive credits from an insurance provider to qualify for insurance ratings.

How Weight Affects Insurance Rates

Insurance companies determine your rating category and therefore the prices you qualify for, based on a build chart similar to that of a BMI. The rating categories include:

- **Preferred Plus:** This is for those who have great health with no history of medical problems.

- **Preferred:** If you have had a minor medical condition or have a family history of moderate conditions, but are in great health, you will probably qualify for this rating.

- **Standard Plus:** This health class includes people with good health but with a negative history in their family or one condition that exempts them from getting a higher rating.

- **Standard:** This is for those with average health that may have some common but manageable health conditions such as blood pressure or high cholesterol.

- **Table Ratings:** It is for high-risk applicants and it is mostly priced according to table ratings. Unless you have a high BMI, it is almost impossible to get a table rating for life insurance based on only your weight.

For each category, a burial insurance giver will have lowest and highest weight limits for a particular height, but your gender and age may also play a role. Some companies apply unisex weight chart, which favors females that may be overweight, since the range of acceptable ratios is higher for men.

Also, other providers take age into account, which favors younger applicants that are overweight, because the ideal weight range for a particular height is broader as you get older.

How Obesity Affects Insurance

Insurance providers care about obesity because obesity is linked to health conditions and can predispose you to many illnesses. The Center for Disease Control and Prevention states that being obese raise your mortality risk for health conditions such as:

- Cancer
- Stroke

- Diabetes
- Kidney disease
- Liver disease
- Heart disease
- High blood pressure
- Sleep apnea
- High cholesterol
- Osteoarthritis

If you have any past health problems due to obesity, the companies offering insurance will demand to know about it before giving you an approved application.

Insurance and Build Charts

A build chart is used as a guideline in the minimum and maximum weight per height by insurance companies. Any insurance company that has a build chart has a section on the application where you will be required to mention your weight and height. However, some insurance companies don't even have charts at all. Other insurance companies build charts that are more lenient than others.

Underwriting Funeral Insurance for Overweight Issues

Underwriting in life insurance aims to know your risk level. Having too much weigh increases a person's risk of having health conditions; this raises the risk of life insurance companies having to pay out earlier than normal.

Underwriting for burial insurance is not the same as traditional life insurance. Traditional term life demands to know your weight because your weight can show your general health. To determine your rate, they will ask about your BMI.

Burial insurance for overweight issues has different underwriting. Some will ask about your weight and height, but even at that, they are lenient with weight issues. However, there are insurance providers without build charts; so, they will not care about your weight.

Factors That May Affect Your Eligibility for Burial Insurance

Overweight individuals are not automatically disqualified from getting cheap burial insurance coverage based on their weight, however, they may be disqualified because of other medical conditions linked to their weight.

Having a recent stroke, cancer, or heart attack, will affect the kind of insurance policy you'll be eligible for and the amount you'll pay. If you any of these conditions, discuss your options with your insurance provider.

Another factor that could affect your eligibility if you're overweight is if you have difficulty walking. If you're too heavy and require assistance in doing your daily activities, you may not qualify for the best burial insurance plan with the best rate. Insurance companies use six daily activities to determine your mobility and decide if you will qualify for first-day coverage. These are:

- **Eating:** using utensils, feeding tube, or intravenously

- **Bathing:** safely washing your body and getting in or out of the shower or bathtub

- **Dressing:** putting on and taking off braces, clothes, fasteners, and prosthesis

- **Toileting:** getting on and off the toilet and performing personal hygiene

- **Transferring:** moving in and out of a chair, bed, or wheelchair

- **Continence:** controlling your bladder and bowel functions

If you are overweight and need help with any of these activities, you'll not be eligible for first-day coverage, even if the provider doesn't have a build chart.

How Obesity Impacts Insurance Costs

Providers will increase premiums if you are significantly obese, but every insurance company has their approach to calculating cost. This makes it hard for people to navigate the insurance marketplace to get cover at good rates.

There are several associated risks and medical complications linked to being obese. It is because of these risks that an insurance provider raises the levels of premium to people who are seen as being obese. The real increase depends on your lifestyle factors, BMI, and medical history.

The process of determining if someone is overweight today is by calculating the Body Mass Index (BMI) of that person. This can be done by dividing their weight by their height. BMI figures are as follows:

- Underweight: less than 17

- Normal: from 18 to 25

- Overweight: from 25 to 30

- Obese: figures from 30 to 40

- Morbidly Obese: higher than 40

Overweight Issues and Burial Insurance Companies

Many burial insurance companies will have their guidelines for weight and height ratio. However, few providers don't weight to height limit at all. You can weigh as much as the whole couch and still qualify for the burial insurance with the lowest premiums. Almost all of the burial insurance companies have low weight limitations. You can be overweight and still you won't get penalized to pay more.

Weight Loss Medications

Currently, there's no prescription drugs that can provide weight loss that can be a concern for insurance companies. You can take any prescribed drug for losing weight, and it will not be a problem with burial insurance providers.

How to Find the Best Burial Insurance for Overweight Issues

Below are some qualities you need to look for in a burial insurance plan and the insurance provider that provides it when concerned about your weight.

- The insurance provider having the lowest monthly premium for a simple plan.

- The provider that gives the best plans for various situations being obese.

- The insurance policy should contain the biggest benefit payment that can immediately protect a person from obesity.

- The burial insurance provider doesn't mind that a person has been hospitalized in the past 12 months.

- The provider should not have a problem with you requiring ADL assistance due to your weight.

PART 3

PUFF PUFF PASS

Insider's Guide to Low Cost Burial Insurance for Those That Use Marijuana

As an Agency, we have assisted many pot smokers in obtaining life insurance at the lowest rate possible. How is this possible for us? It is straightforward. We carry out our homework. We understand the perspective from which all life insurance company view applicants that smokes marijuana.

Also, we know life insurance that is higher in risk and understands what insurance companies love and what they might hate.

As an applicant looking for the lowest life insurance with marijuana, you need to know that working with the right agency will willingly do the hard work and give you the privilege of choosing between many life insurers.

But it would help if you did not worry, as this article will explain how you can get the best life insurer and an affordable rate as an applicant that smokes marijuana or pot smoker. Below is the list of things that we will explain in this article:

- Life insurance plans and marijuana use

- The best life insurer for you if you smoke marijuana

- Choosing the best Agency to get the Best Life insurance rates if you use marijuana.

Life insurance is not an exciting topic. Let's get to the point! Here are the main lessons.

Getting approved and obtaining life insurance as an applicant that uses marijuana, you need to work with life insurers that see marijuana use as being good. All life insurers will want to know how often you use it, whether it's for medications or just for fun. Another thing they will check is whether you have other factors that reconsidered risky in your background.

Life Insurance Plans and Marijuana Use

In my opinion, you will all agree with me that securing life insurance as a marijuana user can be a challenging thing to do. Some life insurance companies will decline you while others will charge you high and others seem unbelievably good.

It is effortless to find the best life insurer if you smoke marijuana. This article will examine the attitudes of some of the leading life insurers towards marijuana smokers.

Life insurance for applicants that smokes marijuana is reduced to their individual use and is part of the life insurer's underwriting.

There are some misconceptions about the attitude of marijuana users towards life insurance. Remember that marijuana does not make you ineligible for getting life insurance. Most life insurers will take out insurance for you.

With this information, we have to ask you questions about your marijuana use in combination with any other health problems. We can find a carrier who may offer life insurance for any medical examination.

The best way to get you the best rates (whether you are a frequent marijuana smoker or you only smoke on occasions) is to help you get a non-smoker rate. The regular smoker rates will make you pay a higher premium.

The Best Life Insurer for You as a Marijuana User

Below are some things that we have found out (carefully examined the italicized Non-smoker)

AIG is formerly known as American General

- If you use marijuana less than two times in a year or just two times, then you can obtain preferred Best *Non-smoker* rates.

- If you only smoke two times in a month or less, you can get a Standard *Non-Smoker.*

- If you use marijuana more than two times in a month, you will be considered a smoker and might get a table rating.

- There must not be THC on your lab report.

Foresters

- Up to 6 times per week for recreational use as standard non-smoker

Legal and General, formerly called Banner Life

- Occasional use will be Standard Smoker.
- If you are an Occasional smoker, you are a Standard smoker.
- If you use marijuana daily, the rate will begin at a substandard Table B smoker.

Mutual of Omaha

- Smoking three times in a month or less is a standard *non-smoker.*
- Between 4 to 8 times in a month will be rated as a case by case

- More than eight times in a month for an individual will be equal to a decline.
- Smoking more than eight times in a month will result in rejection.
- Your lab THC must be equal to the said usage.

Minnesota Life

- If they detect THC in your body, this is a smoke rating in Table 3.
- Both occasional and recreational use at preferred *Non-Smoker*; however, your labs must test negative.
- Twice a month is defined as occasional.

Protective

- The best option is Standard smokers with any amount.
- Depending on the use, the option can be substandard or rejected and whether medical or recreational.

Prudential

- Using marijuana for two times a month and a negative result in laboratories, you will be eligible for standard plus for non-smokers.

- If you use marijuana up to 3 times a week, you will be non-smoking substandard table B (may be positive in laboratories).

Transamerica

- If you use marijuana less than 12 times in a year, you will be eligible for standard non-smoker rates.

- You will be eligible for standard smoker rates if you smoke more than 13 times.

Work with An Independent Agency to Get the Best Life Insurance Rates for Marijuana Users

These are just a few tons of insurers that we have access to. As you can see, this is about including marijuana use in the life insurer's underwriting rules.

First, you want to know if any life insurer is given non-smoking rates, and then compare those rates for each company.

That's why we assist people who smoke marijuana to avoid insurance companies like Prime America, which is only suitable for good health and without potential bad habits.

Contact us, especially if you're looking for a more significant policy, like a $1 million insurance policy; we can help you consider all your options.

If you use marijuana, and your life insurance agent did not do the research we did, contact our agents. We will get the best rate you can be eligible for.

Resources

Aftercare/Grief Services

hollybarker@griefresourcenetwork.com

oceanburial@aol.com (781) 834-0112   Capt. Brad White

clark@memorialkc.com (913) 636-4295

Info@full-circlecare.com (888) 713-4625

Whatsyourgrief@gmail.com (410) 370-6077

Business/Professional Services

shaban@shabanmalikcpa.com (954) 778-7614

mika@tukios.com (801) 682-4391

mustafa.gursoy@maxsold.com (647) 247-5112

info@closurepath.com (855)-Per-Path

Caskets

Info@cherokeespecialtycaskets.com (800) 535-8667

Clearviewcaskets.com (888) 305-8439

Cremations

Simplecremationonline.com (866) 333-5130

Customercare@thumbies.com (877) 848-6243

Eco-Friendly Burial

sales@passagesinternational.com (505) 830-2500 Drew Lara

kinkaraco@gmail.com (415) 874-9698   Esmerelda Kent

Katieboehm@memorialreefs.international (808) 345-0184

mclemire@musesdesign.com (514) 318-7122

ctcaskets.com (860)786-7687

Eulogy Writing

Petra@beloved-press.com (248) 894-7076

Family Tree

Info@familychartmasters.com (801) 872-4278

Floral Arrangements & Preservation

Floristone.com (888) 610-8262

Flowersforcemeteries.com (770) 428-8883

Info@timelessmoments.com (440) 523-1099

Funeral Directories

Affordablefuneralsnetworkafn@gmail.com www.afnfunerals.com
(800) 750-2766

Hologram Memorials

Cminardo@aimholographics.com (609)923-2286   Carl
Minardo/Steve Harless

Memorial Products

Laura@lpcameos.com (416) 386-1752

Memorymedallion.com (877) 418-8107

Berylmartin.com (219) 545-2129

Tshirtstotreasures@tshirtstotreasures.com (843)810-0940 Cheryl

kelly@cloverlawnbutterflies.com (407) 896-8389

Obituary Provider

hello@beyondthedash.com (877) 830-5330 Brigitte Ganger

Planning Process

info@remembranceprocess.com

Remains Return Protection

Support@sepioguard.com (877) 625-2726

Rosaries

Paula@familyrosaries.com (978) 221-6326   Paula Barbieri-Stewart

Rosfromflowers@aol.com (978) 851-9103

Diane@wrightkeepsakesandjewelry.com (508) 397-5531

Supplies & Memorials

Eli@americanmemorycraft.com (541) 890-8934

Spiritpieces@gmail.com (914) 924-5120 David Blake

cg@sficromo.com (818) 547-1390 Carlos George

service@newmemorialsdirect.com (253) 649-0568 Michelle Bailey

heloisa@laralaserworks.com (714) 749-8510

Cherishedkps.com (617) 971-8590

info@claritymemories.com (800) 697-0725

Cremaingem.com (408) 390 8954

Info@gracefulburial.com (651) 246-1133

Dnabanking@preventiongenetics.com (715) 387-0484

Info@preciousvesseljewelry.com (888) 515-8324

Mail@loveisarose.com (630) 393-1111

Space Memorials

info@mesoloft.com (502) 275-1413

Celestis.com (281) 971-4019 Gary Gartner

Urns

Alviti.com (800) 888-8258

Amaranthineurns.com (610) 443-0124

klongendyke@terrybear.com (651) 352-2296 Kelcy Longendyke

customerservice@timberlandurns.com (651) 688-0875 Val Grinshpun

sales@americanmadeurns.com (918) 331-8766 William Brummett

salesdept@rajindia.com (800) 845-3665 Jeff

Info@bonsaiurn.com (628) 259-2162

blake@chateauurns.com (888) 536-5450

Info@capsuleproject.com (360) 513-3475 Steve Prastka

Info@cpurns.com (503) 593-7490

Info@foreverence.com (888) 730-6111

Eternitrees.com (866) 828-4841

biourn4pets@gmail.com (877) 370-1166

Sales@shivashade.com (516) 665-8325

Vaults

Info@doric-vaults.com (888) 55-Doric

Info@clarkvault.com (800) 848-3570

Author Bio

Since 1986 financial expert Al Kushner has helped thousands of individuals, families, and business owners use cash value life insurance to build wealth and find financial peace of mind. He makes the complex world of insurance and financial services simple to understand so that people feel empowered to take control of their financial lives. As the Founder and President of Superior Mutual Inc, Al and his team help many to preserve, protect and pass on a legacy. He is a warm and gifted communicator who has a passion for helping particularly seniors keep more of what they have worked a lifetime to save. For more information call 888-810-9725 or visit SuperiorMutual.com

How to Save Up to 90% Off Your Prescriptions

Free Rx Prescription Drug Card

Save Up to 90% OFF your prescriptions

✳ Free For Everyone   ✳ Discounts in Brand and Generic Medications
✳ No Restrictions   ✳ HIPAA Compliant

Walgreens   Winn✓Dixie   Walmart
Kroger   ◎ TARGET   COSTCO WHOLESALE

✳ Bring to Pharmacy   ✳ Give Card to Pharmacist   ✳ Save!

FREE Prescription Discount Card

Card is Active. Call or go online now for program details.

Member ID # DDN7073
BIN # 015558
Group # DDN7073

Member Info: 877.537.5537
www.ddnrxsavings.com/DDN7073

Discount Program | This is not insurance   powered by ◎ Discount Drug Network

Welcome to Your Free Prescription Discount Card, lowest overall prices at most chains, HIPAA compliant, and no mail order offerings that compete with pharmacies or agents! Save 14% to 21% on Brand, and sometimes over 90% on generics, depending on what medication you are prescribed!

DDNRX Patient's benefit: We have the highest overall savings of any other card in the market; this means the lowest overall prices on prescription drugs. There is no need to shop around; with this card they receive the same low price at every participating pharmacy. Use your favorite chain Pharmacy and keep using them with comfort that you are receiving the lowest price available. Patients Information is NEVER disclosed or sold to any third party, nor released to anyone for any purpose. DDNRx Free Prescription Discount Card is HIPAA compliant.

Save 10 - 90% off all your prescriptions
Everyone is Approved
Instant Activation
No Pre-Existing Conditions
No Waiting Periods
Never Expires
The card is free, you are paying for shipping.
You don't need a physical card to use it. Just show the picture to your pharmacist.

You can even write it down. What is important is the

BIN:015558
Member ID # DDN7073
Group: DDN7073 ********Must have correct group to use!!

My Gift to You!

Thank you for purchasing this book. As a token of my appreciation, I'm giving you a FREE 40-page special report:

Colonial Penn, Globe Life, Lincoln Heritage, Mutual of Omaha & AARP Burial Insurance – Are These Companies A Rip-Off?

Discover the secrets that they don't want you to know in my free special report now!

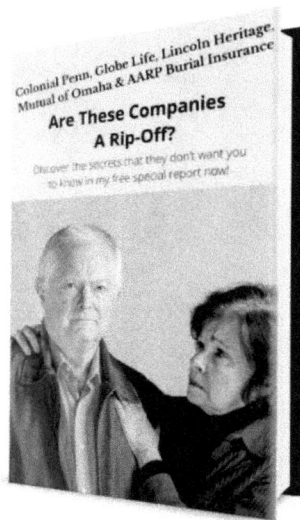

Get it here at https://BookHip.com/XLBBNX

or scan qr code below

www.ingramcontent.com/pod-product-compliance
Lightning Source LLC
Chambersburg PA
CBHW060309030426
42336CB00011B/982